MYSTICAL ROSE

MARY, PARADIGM OF THE RELIGIOUS LIFE

THOMAS PHILIPPE, O.P.

Our Sunday Visitor Publishing Division
Our Sunday Visitor, Inc.
Huntington, Indiana 46750

The book cover, designed by Rebecca J. Heaston, takes its inspiration from a stained-glass window in St. Anthony's Church, South Bend, Indiana. The work of the artist Anthony Panzicka, this window is devoted to the Mystical Rose. Thanks are also due to Rev. Richard Bullene, C.S.C., and Dr. Robert Ringel, architects at the University of Notre Dame, for their suggestions, and for Dr. Ringel's photographs which were used in designing the cover.

The icon of the "Unfading Rose" found on page 18 is the work of Sharon Gill.

649

Dedicated to the community of La Ferme

Table of Contents

Preface

A word must be said in explanation of the complex authorship of this book. The substance comes entirely from Father Thomas Philippe, a French Dominican who taught philosophy and theology for many years at the faculties of Saulchoir (in Belgium, then in France) and the Angelicum (in Rome). He is not primarily an academic, however; preaching and spiritual direction have always been at the forefront of his ministry. Even on the academic side, his interest centered chiefly on spiritual theology.

He was ordained in 1929, and the first years of his ministry took place in the period when the Catholic Action movement was developing in Belgium and France. He was in direct contact with the leaders of the JOC (Young Christian Workers) and JAC (Young Christian Farmers), particularly Canon Cardijn and the Abbés Guerin and Gorlin. In collaborating with them, he was struck by the fact that the Holy Spirit seemed to work more profoundly and interiorly in milieux touched by poverty and suffering — namely, among the laborers and farmers, than among university people.

The appearance in French of the writings of Freud and Jung led Father Philippe to give his attention to the "psychoanalytic revolution." During the late forties and early fifties, he worked in conjunction with Doctor John Thompson, a Canadian psychiatrist on the staff of UNESCO in Paris. A former assistant to Freud, and a personal friend of Jung and of Aldous Huxley, Thompson had recently entered the Catholic Church. In conversations with him, Father Philippe began to probe the depths of human consciousness and the subconscious, seeking for the natural foundations of the theological virtues and the gifts of the Holy Spirit.

Obliged by illness and deafness to give up teaching, he devoted himself to the pastoral care of the retarded, the mentally ill and in fact almost every sort of handicapped or ill-adapted person. His own infirmities, under the light of the Holy Spirit, gave him a kind of connatural understanding of such people. Since 1964 he was chaplain of

L'Arche. This extraordinary work, founded in the little village of Trosly-Breuil by Jean Vanier, has the handicapped living together in small communities with the people who care for them. Father Philippe stayed in Trosly-Breuil as a theologian-apostle of the Holy Spirit, but even more as a father to the poor, and to all who are in misery. This ministry was like an extension of that on which he had embarked as a young professor with Canon Cardijn and Abbé Godin. He was likewise an apostle of Mary, the *poorest* of Jesus' disciples (as this book will explain) and likewise the one who most completely surrendered to the Holy Spirit.

Severely impaired as the result apparently of a stroke, he spent the last two years of his life handicapped, like those to whom he had always ministered so lovingly. He died on February 4, 1993, while this manuscript was waiting to be printed.

Except for a few articles in journals of theology and spirituality, Father Philippe did not publish much. The chief instruments of his apostolate were the word and personal presence. From the beginning of his priesthood, he experienced a need to nourish his spirit by direct contact with Jesus and the poor — in other words, by prayerful contemplation and apostolic ministry. Although many urged him to do more writing, he never had much time to do so. Furthermore, at a deeper level, he always hesitated to write for fear that a written text would give too fixed a form to his thought, which is forever living, groping and expressing itself in new ways. He was reluctant even to reread and correct his own texts or the notes taken by others on his conferences. He sought to keep himself always free and responsive to the living touch of human reality, and even more, obedient to the Holy Spirit, the sole interior master of his heart.

Nevertheless, those who esteem Father Philippe's teaching, and want to make it better known, have for years been circulating notes and transcriptions of his conferences, with his consent. At first, they used a mimeograph; then, with the aid of a press, small editions were printed at La Ferme (60350 Trosly-Breuil, France). Just in the last few years, larger editions have been brought out by Éditions St.-Paul, Le Lion de Juda and other Catholic publishing houses in France. Two of his works have appeared thus far in English: *The Fire of Contemplation* (Alba House, New York, 1981) and *The Contemplative Life* (Crossroads, New York, 1990). Translations of several others are in preparation.

The present work originated in some notes composed about 1960 under the title *Marie, modèle de la vie religieuse* ("Mary, model of the religious life"). They were rearranged and abridged in a small book, *La vie cachée de Marie* ("The hidden life of Mary") by Dominique Montfort, a faithful disciple and longtime secretary of Father Philippe. This work has been published in two small editions by La Ferme.

I began by translating *La vie cachée*, comparing it, however, with the original text, which I have restored in many instances. Moreover, I had the opportunity to verify, complete and refine many points through personal conversations with Father Philippe himself. With his full consent, I have acted, not just as translator, but as an editor of the text, making such adaptations, rearrangements and clarifications as seemed advisable for English-language readers. The appendices are entirely my work; so also are the footnotes, except for a few indicated by the initials T.P. I wrote some brief introductory paragraphs for chapters 1, 8, 10 and 13. Finally, I have made occasional slight rearrangements and interpolations in the text. The latter have been drawn largely from other works or spoken comments of Father Philippe; on a few points, they are modest attempts to relate his reflections to the results of modern historical studies. In all cases this has been done in a spirit of total loyalty to his teaching, and with the motive of making it more accessible. (The more important interpolations are indicated by the use of italics, but it would have been too complicated to do this for the minor ones.)

One might wonder why the translation is not based directly on the original text of *Marie, modèle de la vie religieuse*. The answer is that its style — complex, disorganized and repetitious — would probably keep many readers from ever discovering the profound wisdom shrouded by it. Father Philippe along with his closest friends agreed that his work needed revision; but the few times he attempted to do this himself resulted in a substantially new text that still needed editing as much as the original! Generally speaking, I don't like for texts to be edited by someone other than the author; but in this case, there seemed no other solution.

What is there in Father Philippe's teaching that motivates people to go to so much trouble to disseminate it? This is something very difficult to put into words. Briefly, I would say that it is the fruit of profound personal mystical experience, with an extraordinary power to foster the spiritual life of others.

I have no doubt that some readers will find here instead an uninteresting mélange of subtle scholasticism and ingenuous piety. Let me therefore explain as well as I can, first, that it is certainly not literary style that makes this work remarkable. There is in the Church a long tradition of sacred eloquence, in which great natural gifts have been put at the service of the Gospel, and the beauties of human speech used to alert people to the beauties of the Kingdom of God. Such is not the gift of Father Philippe, despite the fact that he is the nephew and disciple of Thomas-Pierre Dehau, O.P., whose magnificent intelligence, artistic sensitivity and eloquence produced some of the finest French spiritual writing of the present century. Although Father Dehau had a powerful influence on the intellectual formation of his nephew, his rhetorical gifts were not transmitted.

Father Philippe had a power to touch and change the hearts of those who heard him. It was above all a gift of the spoken word, though it extended to his writing also. However, it was not by rhetoric, but as a sheer instrument of grace, that he accomplished this. He was not like St. Ambrose, whose eloquence was admired even by those who had no interest in his message.

Secondly, it is not erudition that gives Father Philippe's work its value. He was not very *au courant* of contemporary theological and exegetical movements. His knowledge of history, even Church history and the history of spirituality, was meager by comparison with the learned authorities in these fields. His was a mind that reflected deeply on the meaning of a few facts, rather than being a storehouse of them.

Thirdly, it is not even primarily for its theological quality that this work deserves to be read. Father Philippe was a very competent theologian formed in the Neo-Thomism of the French Dominicans between the two World Wars — a school represented by Sertillanges, Gardeil and Garrigou-Lagrange. The intellectualism of this type of theology strikes many people today as ill-suited to the articulation of the mysteries of faith; in any case it makes for very difficult reading. But the theological method employed is, if not irrelevant to, at least incommensurable with, the true value of this book. One who is not at home with scholastic metaphysics can still profit greatly from the text, if only he has the patience to get used to its idiom.

Father Philippe did not disdain theology; he took it very seriously as a means of exploring, articulating and defending the faith on which all Christian spirituality is based. Nevertheless, as a spiritual guide, he is engaged in a work that far transcends the idiom in which it is expounded. (In this respect, he closely resembles St. John of the Cross.)

Even the mystical doctrine found here will probably disappoint people avid for original mystical insights. It has little in common with the "speculative mysticism" of that other Dominican theologian from St.-Jacques, Meister Eckhart. It is a mysticism of poverty and littleness, not only in its recommendations, but in style and mode. It does not regard mystical experience as the achievement of an intense and genial spirit, but as a gift received without merit by those who are simple and little enough to live in the company of Jesus and Mary.

I do not want to give the impression that Father Philippe is the kind of person who goes through life operating with no other intellectual instruments than those he learned at school. He is almost the polar opposite of that: ever reflecting, reformulating his ideas, taking a fresh look at reality. I know of no one else so sensitive and acute in understanding human psychology.

His discernment of spirits was not the product of academic study so much as the work of grace and the fruit of an extraordinary ability to be totally present and sympathetic to each person with whom he spoke. Nevertheless, ever since his early contact with the thought of Freud and Jung, he remained in lively communication with contemporary French psychologists. On another plane, without being in any sense a scientist himself, he kept in touch with the perspectives of science through regular conversations with his close friend, the oceanographer Xavier Le Pichon. Economists, political scientists, social workers and philosophers (most notably Jacques Maritain) were among his associates. An immense burden of spiritual direction and counseling left him little time to read; but he was an exceptionally gifted conversationalist in the land where the art of conversation is more highly cultivated than anywhere else in the world. These conversations enriched him immensely (as they never failed to be enriched by his contributions). He was interested in everything but trivia (and even in apparently trivial matters, he often discerned a significance overlooked by others). He was most of all interested in people — all people, but particularly the suffering, the marginalized and the handicapped, whom he regarded as his chief teachers under the Holy Spirit.

But however they were acquired, intellectual riches are not displayed in the following pages, except for occasional flashes of psychological insight or cosmic perspective. What is more apparent is a kind of poverty that some will find disappointing. But it is the magnanimous poverty of one who sold all he had in order to purchase the pearl of great price; who counted everything else as loss compared to the surpassing greatness of knowing Jesus Christ. Father Philippe does not write or speak to share his cultural riches with others, but to help them open up to the God who hides his secrets from the wise and learned, and reveals them to little ones.

Finally, some readers may be disturbed by theoretical positions taken or assumed here: the emphasis on littleness, passivity and interiority; the immense role attributed to Mary in the plan of salvation, and at the same time the affirmation of her poverty of memory and imagination, dependence on Joseph and lack of personal initiative; the 'old-fashioned' notion of the role of woman in the family and in society. These views stand against the prevailing currents of psychology, sociology and spirituality, but it would take far too long to discuss them here. I have tried to deal with some of them in the Supplementary Notes. About the rest, I can only affirm that Father Philippe's views are the prayerfully pondered judgments of a man who had an extraordinary deep and rich experience of human life touched by divine grace. I would urge the reader, when he finds them outrageous, not to dismiss them out of hand, but to give them the serious, respectful consideration due to a man of tested wisdom. Even one who cannot accept them as they stand will find much truth in them. And they might lead him eventually to a completely new perspective on the universe.

"My thoughts are not your thoughts, neither are your ways my ways, declares the Lord" (Isaiah 55:8). But there are chosen disciples to whom the Lord is pleased to reveal the secrets of his Kingdom; and those who have not been privileged to lean upon the Master's breast are wise when they learn from those who have.

* * *

Several people read this work while it was in preparation, and helped me by their observations: Father Bernard Mullahy, C.S.C., former professor of spiritual theology at Regina Mundi Institute, Rome; Dr. Eugene Campanale, associate professor at St. Mary's College, Notre Dame, and a specialist in developmental psychology; Sister Amata Fabbro, O.P., chairman of the theology department at Aquinas College, Grand Rapids; Sister Verda Clare, C.S.C., former Provincial of the Midwest Province of the Sisters of the Holy Cross; and Carmine Buonaiuto, a former graduate student at the University of Notre Dame.

Publication of the work was greatly facilitated by a generous grant from Mr. James Byrne.

The typing was done by Mrs. Cheryl Reed, Mrs. Bobbi Thompson, and Mrs. Nancy Kegler of the Faculty Steno Pool at Notre Dame, with generous assistance also from

Mrs. Bert Kovacsics and Mrs. Alma McLane. Sister Mary Jeremy, O.P., of Rosary College located the text of St. Gertrude cited in chapter 4.

My sincerest thanks to them all.

Edward D. O'Connor, C.S.C.

Introduction

In some ways, our age is propitious to the contemplative life; in other ways, quite the contrary. Certainly our scientific and technological achievements are not always a sure help to union with God. More often than not, they tend to diminish our faith in Providence and draw us away from the spirit of Jesus, especially from prayer and sacrifice. The movement of today's world seems to be taking mankind farther and farther away from God and the Gospel. In complicity with our own concupiscence, it has produced a materialistic civilization, philosophies of life and secular humanisms that contradict the humility, poverty, docility and sacrifice inculcated by the Gospel.

Without insisting on grosser errors and seductions, let us note that the economic and social conditions of modern culture, as well as its psychological climate, create very practical difficulties for the spiritual life. For example, the dominance of economic factors leads to a more and more complex system of laws, which in turn makes administration more complicated and demanding. This weighs heavily on the life of religious communities by absorbing the time, attention and energies of superiors in a veritable slavery.

At the same time, modern equipment and appliances have become indispensable to religious houses. No doubt, they save time and energy which can be devoted to contemplation. They also make religious life possible for people not strong enough to endure the austerity of the ancient monasteries. They enable us to provide some of the necessities of life for ourselves, which is quite in accord with the spirit of poverty. But is there not a serious danger of their detracting from the simplicity, poverty and sacrifice which should be the atmosphere of religious houses? Under the cover of modern technology and all that accompanies it, may not the spirit of the world, with its prejudices, myths of progress, etc., insinuate itself?

On another plane, modern psychology fosters a mentality that profoundly undermines the religious life and, for that matter, any genuine interior life. It inclines us (unconsciously perhaps) to look at things primarily from a human and psychological point of view, rather than from that of supernatural faith and charity. At the same time, a vast body of contemporary literature is devoted to the cultivation of self. It aims, to be sure, not at a grossly self-parading ego, but at a deep, refined self — one that takes a kind of aesthetic pleasure in the scrutiny of its own inner experience. It delights to turn in upon itself and analyze itself. But this seductive, cultivated self which can easily take on the appearance of virtue remains nevertheless an ego — something which has to die before one can enter into a truly intimate relationship with Jesus. The ego is the greatest obstacle to the spirit of littleness presupposed by such intimacy. And the grosser forms of egotism are often less dangerous in this regard than the refined ones, because so obvious and hence more humiliating.

But with all its problems, our age can be seen, when viewed with the eyes of faith, to enjoy certain graces and spiritual resources not available in the past. Two in particular must be cited here: on the one hand, the dogmatic definitions of the Immaculate Conception and Assumption, along with the whole development of Marian theology and spirituality stimulated by them; on the other hand, the emphasis on childlikeness, littleness, simplicity and interior poverty by which the modern saints and mystics have brought about a real deepening of spiritual life in the Church. It is they who have most insisted, either by their writings or by example, on interior poverty and the spirit of littleness, which providentially is possible for those whose frail health obliges them to mitigate the traditional asceticism. Saints such as Thérèse of Lisieux have made us aware of the heroism of littleness, which consists essentially in the constant mortification of memory, imagination, reason and all the senses, in order to attack the evil at its root, where Mary's little ones, abiding in the presence of their God, are able to overcome it.

The spirit of littleness is rooted in devotion to the Sacred Heart of Jesus and to the Blessed Virgin Mary; that is to say, in a profound and intimate participation in the hidden life of Jesus and Mary. Hence it seems possible to summarize the peculiar grace of modern times thus: the Church (and through it the Holy Spirit himself) has led us to Mary, and she in turn best teaches us how to be little ones in the way called for by the Gospel.

A kind of divine equilibrium requires that the bigness characteristic of so many aspects of modern civilization be counterbalanced by an equivalent development in littleness. Mary is the only one who can teach us the docility to the Holy Spirit necessary to bring this about. In a world inclined to measure things by size, and on the spatial and temporal scale of the universe, she teaches the wisdom of littleness and of abiding humbly in the present moment. Only thus can we discover the eternal in every place and time, and abide in divine love.

The difficulties which the spiritual life encounters today, particularly as regards its equilibrium and the abnegation it requires, are such that the classical masters of spirituality, valid though their doctrine remains, no longer provide us with sufficient guidance. But at the same time, a kind of divine compensation is giving us the opportunity of direct recourse to the one whose Immaculate Conception placed her at the very fountainhead of all spiritual life. Though living by faith as we do, she had a uniquely intimate relationship with Jesus and the Holy Spirit, such as no other saint even approached.

Marian spirituality is characterized by a close union of doctrine and practice. It is very objective, because based directly on the dogmas of the Church, especially the two recently defined ones. At the same time, it is a spirituality of littleness and of personal intimacy with Jesus and Mary. Mary teaches us how to be little ones abiding in the presence of our God, and her radiant presence prevents the spirit of the world from permeating us.

Thus it is in view of the obligations and responsibilities, opportunities and difficulties, of the present era, that we wish to speak about the mystery of the Immaculate Virgin, especially her hidden life, and what may be called her religious life — the life of poverty, humility, virginity and silence — which she led, first with St. Joseph, and later on with Jesus. We would like to meditate on Mary with the reader, or better, pass some time with him close to her, reflecting on certain aspects of her life and on that mystery which makes her our model in a special way. She herself will know how to suggest, deep in the heart of each, gently but firmly, the practical resolutions required for a better knowledge of, and greater intimacy with, her Immaculate Heart.

May these pages be an occasion for her to visit each of our hearts, bringing joy and encouragement. May she make us understand better how our life ought to be a response, under her tutelage, to the call to prayer and penance that has been the theme of her message at La Salette, Lourdes, Fátima and many other places. When we grant her full freedom to visit us in the depths of our hearts, she will make us understand that the prayer of silence, which was the very life of her soul, and which she desires above all from her contemplatives, is the adequate response to this request. For this prayer involves a union of love consummated in a total gift of self, which here below always entails sacrifice.

* * *

We begin with the Immaculate Conception, a grace which placed Mary from the outset at a height toward which the saints tend without ever fully reaching it. This is the state of loving union with God into which the graces of the unitive life plunge the mystic more and more deeply. It is also the state of an infant who stays ever close to its Heavenly Father. Here, we will see why Mary was the *least* as well as the greatest of all the saints, and the model *par excellence* of the spirituality of littleness.

Next we will examine this spirituality of littleness and intimacy with God which sprang from her state. We will see how it inspired her to choose a mode of life that was hidden and silent, comparable to the religious life in the Church today. This life prepared her for the Annunciation, in which it culminated.

The Annunciation was like a new birth for Mary. By an invisible mission of the Holy Spirit, the infant Jesus was given to her as the child of her love. But this required her to begin life all over again in a new spirit of littleness, as a pupil of her divine infant who was infinitely more 'little' than herself.

From the hidden, silent life of the Holy Family at Nazareth, Jesus went forth to proclaim the Gospel to the world; but the prayer and sacrifice of the hidden life continued to envelope the exterior activities of his public life. When, at Jesus' cross, Mary was given to John and through him to the Church, it was in order to perpetuate there that same hidden life, which keeps the Church united to Jesus, in the likeness of Mary. By it likewise the Church is the bride of Jesus and the mother of men. The two great duties of prayer and sacrifice — so often neglected today — are the essential means by which the Holy Spirit prepared, in and through Mary, for the coming of Jesus. Mary reminds us that the eternal, unchanging wisdom of the Holy Spirit is completing the work of Jesus in the world today by these same two means of prayer and penance.

Finally, we will learn from the hidden life of Mary that the world returns to God, not along the dimension of earthly grandeur, but along that new dimension of the littleness and intimacy of love which only the Holy Spirit can make us discover.

Part One

♣

The Foundations of Mary's Spirituality

CHAPTER 1

The Initial State of the Life of Grace in Mary

Human nature bears deep within itself a mysterious leaven of sin, the baleful fermentation of which taints everything we do. The grace of the Immaculate Conception implies that the Mother of Jesus was the sole person, besides her Son, whose nature was untouched by sin. This privilege had enormous consequences for the development of Mary's life. It gave her an attitude, a mentality, a consciousness profoundly different from that of all the rest of humanity. The difference can be expressed to some degree even in psychological terms.

Libido or Love?

Freud holds that the basic and initial impulse of human psychology is what he calls libido. All other forms of human motivation, from the grossest lust to the noblest idealism, arise as modulations or sublimations of this original instinct. The Freudian libido, however, seems to be in reality the selfishness of a somewhat older child retrojected upon the infant. On theological and philosophical grounds, especially in a Christian perspective, it would seem rather that the initial attitude of an infant is one of love. The analysis of human affectivity by St. Thomas Aquinas shows that love has to be the first affective movement of the soul; even cupidity presupposes love.[1] Furthermore, the first movement of the human soul comes from God who, in creating it, imparts its initial dynamism. Hence the first human act (like the first act of the angel) can only be good, and cannot be anything other than love.[2]

Providence has arranged that the newborn human, unlike the young of other animals, is quite unable to provide the basic necessities of life for itself. Consequently, it has a completely dependent relationship to its mother. Nevertheless, it is a true human being. The deep and lasting consequences of the child's very first behavior on its future life, even on its spiritual activities, is a sign that its psychological activity from the beginning was not confined to the sensory level but was already fully immersed in and enveloped by the spiritual. (The spirituality in this case is, of course, purely natural.)

Secondly, the infant's first contacts with its mother occur prior to the exercise of imagination and the other internal senses, and even before the use of sight. They involve only the sense of touch, which is exercised with a purity, simplicity and depth it will never know again. Moreover, the imagination has not yet begun to intervene in the act of sensation to color and interpret it. On the other hand, the mind and will are directly involved. Their first awareness of existence and of things comes about, in a very concrete and sensory way, through this act of touch.[3] Out of this eminently vital and 'substantial' exercise of the sense of touch, nothing but love can arise directly.

The infant's initial love for its mother, as it becomes conscious, is direct and objective, involving no reflection upon the self that would justify the appraisal selfish crudely and thoughtlessly imposed upon it by many psychologists. Since the fall of Adam, however, this first natural love, though utterly pure in essence, is extremely weak and imperfect. Because of original sin, we are born deprived of grace. Our nature, which was like matter disposed for the reception of grace, is profoundly affected by this privation. It is said to be 'wounded,' even though its natural substance is not corrupted.

Hence the infant does not remain permanently in the attitude in which it was placed by the Creator at the beginning of its life. It bears in its body a heritage of sin, the virtualities of which quickly begin to be realized, impelling it to abandon that initial attitude of love. When the child's faculties have developed sufficiently for it to become aware of its surroundings and to begin to want to act and move by itself, it is no longer content with that first natural love, which was very weak and was directed explicitly only toward its mother. A host of contrary tendencies arise, which this love is not strong enough to surmount and master. They tend to crystallize at a level inferior to love, thereby creating the *ego* — the conscious subject that seeks to relate everything to itself as the center and goal.

Furthermore, the family and the whole milieu within which this new life has to develop, are also marked by the consequences of the fall. The mother's natural affection lacks the purity, delicacy and generosity necessary to respond suitably to the expectations of the infant's initial love. She often disappoints her child, even without knowing it. The latter feels neglected, abandoned, misunderstood; hence its tears and anxiety (which are so different, however, from the cry of an animal!). Little by little, the infant's first love for its mother loses the character of complete trust and self-surrender. Reactions of defense against anxiety make their contribution to the formation of the ego, which will supplant the initial love.

Of course the child retains a deep affection for its mother, but this affection no longer has the directness and totality of perfect love, at least not in an actual and conscious way. Although suppressed from direct consciousness, the initial love remains in a latent and subconscious form. It continues to inspire that deep affection by which the child naturally trusts and hopes in its parents, teachers, the community and nature itself, all of which encompass and mold it. In fact, up to the moment when the child has to choose for itself the ultimate goal of life, these deep affections, confirmed and stabilized by the authority and affection of its parents, keep the child tending toward the natural goals of human life. They prevail over the contrary tendencies of the ego and maintain an orientation to God.

There is a struggle going on, however, between the ego and these higher aspirations. The former, impatient and aggressive, constantly seeking to relate everything to itself, is uppermost in the child's consciousness. The latter, which incline the child to take its part humbly and lovingly in a common life broader than itself, and in this way orient it toward its last end, are more passive and more latent.

The Life of Grace: A New Birth

In the life of grace, and under the action of the Holy Spirit, the adult recovers the attitudes of faith, trust and familial affection natural to the infant; but this time they are adopted freely, consciously and supernaturally. The proper goal of the 'illuminative way'[4] is to develop in us that childlikeness which consists in a faith and hope fully illumined and inspired by the gifts of the Holy Spirit.

However, the illuminative way does more than make us keep the law of God in a filial spirit. By its profound inspiration, arising directly from love, it tends to draw us closer and closer to God, so that we may live in his presence, in intimate union with him, through the graces of quiet and union.[5] In other words, the illuminative life prepares the way for the unitive. It tends toward its own consummation in the union and gift of love.

After all the passive purifications and privations undergone by the reason, intelligence and memory; after — or rather in close conjunction with — the death of the ego, there occurs very truly a *new birth*, in which, through total trust and absolute self-surrender, a person recovers that original attitude of love which as an infant he had had for his mother. But before regaining the unfailing trust of an infant, one must experience again, in the form of real agony, those anxieties of the infant which were at the origin of the ego. One's life will be divided, perhaps for a long period of time, between moments of completely trustful love and moments of horrible abandonment, without any of those intermediary attitudes that had developed 'naturally' under the drive of the ego, and which go to make up what is regarded as ordinary and normal human psychology.

Thus we can see that, under the inspiration of the Holy Spirit, the life of grace develops in the opposite direction from the tendency of the ego. Instead of allowing us to drift downstream, the Holy Spirit obliges us to go back upstream, beyond all the contaminations which life has brought us, to that utterly pure spring of life coming directly from God. Underneath all the deformations of sin and all our miserable 'acquisitions,' He uncovers this authentic source of life within us.

Mary's Love as an Infant

In the Blessed Virgin Mary, however, things were different. In her, grace was in a sense prior to nature because, unlike all the rest of mankind, she was conceived in the state of grace. Due to this unique mode of her sanctification, charity was already being exercised in her before the genesis of an ego. The first movement of her psychic life was not merely a weak and imperfect natural love directed toward her mother alone, but a supernatural love, strong and perfect, one which was already, in a sense, a fullness. Her initial grace was truly *royal*, suited to the Queen of the Universe, who had been placed higher than all angels and men by God's predestination.

In Mary, the infant's first love for its mother was supernaturalized by grace. Her love was not that barely conscious love found in other infants, which does not extend explicitly beyond the person of the mother. Materially it was like that of other infants, yet with an essential difference. Like theirs it was an extremely simple form of love devoid of any input from reason or imagination; but it already entailed a very strong contact with God. In and through the person of her mother, Mary's love attained God himself directly and properly. From the very outset of her life, Mary loved God 'as a mother' infinitely more than she loved her natural mother, however good the latter may have been. This love filled Mary's infant heart to overflowing, and she sought nothing outside of it. Never would she try, even for a second, or by any stray impulse of her imagination, to escape from the sweet and powerful ascendancy of the love which united her to the Holy Spirit, thereby placing her from birth in the very bosom of the Adorable Trinity.

Thus the earthly life of the Immaculate Virgin began at the peak of the unitive way, a peak of which the greatest saints barely catch glimpses toward the end of their lives, when their ego has finally been put to death through mortifications and trials of all sorts.

Ordinarily, charity makes its first appearance as the inspiration of other human activities. At a higher stage of development, it is exercised not only in activities, but also in passive states or attitudes. At first transitory, these states tend to become more and more continuous and profound in the saints and to remain, at least in a latent form, even when activity is being carried on. Finally, this love, passive in itself but capable of inspiring and suffusing all activities, becomes a kind of permanent and spontaneous state, in which the natural attitude of the infant is recovered.

In the Queen of Saints, charity was present from the first instant of her earthly existence with incomparable purity and plenitude, even though in a form proportionate to an infant. Throughout the rest of her life, we can say that it remained forever the same, yet never ceased to grow deeper and more intense. Mary is the saint who made the greatest progress in love. There is an almost infinite distance between the degree of her grace the day she was born and that which she attained at the Assumption. There were no halfhearted acts in her life; each act was more fervent than any of those preceding it. The development of grace in her took place, not just by a continuous rise, unbroken by any descents or delays, but by a continual sequence of new 'ascensions' inspired by the Holy Spirit. Nevertheless her initial love was always there, inspiring and enveloping all her activities and her whole life, physical as well as psychic, in its human aspects as well as those of grace.

The language of human psychology is unable to express this mystery. It even falsifies it, because Mary did not have the sense of self that is usual in human psychology. She did not have an 'ego' as psychologists speak of it. Her consciousness was stabilized at a deeper level by the Holy Spirit, prior to the origin of the ego. This gave her what we might call a *mystical* consciousness, which was more profound, more intimate and more vigorous than the sense of self in any other human being. This mystical consciousness derived its stability, not from any intellectual light, but from a supernatural love that was, as it were, incarnate in her being. This is the key to the life of her Immaculate Heart.

CHAPTER 2

The Characteristic Notes
of Mary's Spirituality

We must now try to define the essential characteristics which made Mary's mystical consciousness so utterly different from the psychological consciousness of the human ego. Like all of us, including Jesus himself, she grew in wisdom and age. Her mind, her will, her affectivity and sensitivity, all developed, but in a very different way from ours.

Our ego, being at the origin of our whole psychic dynamism, imprints two fundamental traits on the latter: 1) a *self-centeredness* which constantly turns us back upon ourselves so that we tend to draw everything to ourselves, to 'collect' things and, in Marcel's sense, to 'have' them; and 2) an *activism* which, on the one hand, seeks to impose itself aggressively on everyone and everything and, on the other hand, constantly seeks its own ease and pleasure. Hence our ego is a bundle of three selfish drives or instincts: 1) a desire to *possess*, which imprints a characteristic psychological note even on the activities of our mind; 2) a desire to *dominate*, which biases the activity of the will; and 3) a craving for *pleasure*, which contaminates our whole sensual life.

In Mary, love, rather than such an ego, unified everything and imparted its spirit and orientation to her entire life. Instead of a self-consciousness it gave her a consciousness focused on her Beloved. Her attitude was one of loving passivity, eager to be loved, and at the same time ready to respond to love with an offering and effective sacrifice of self.

The ego implies self-will, self-love, 'having a mind of one's own'; in short, *egotism.* Love implies poverty, humility and docility, purity of heart and sacrifice. Let us examine these notes (which, incidentally, lie at the origin of the evangelical counsels of poverty, chastity and obedience).

Poverty of Spirit

Instead of that proprietary instinct which appears very early in a child's life, making it take possession of people and things for itself, Mary had a spirit of poverty. She was free from that need to amass a treasure of images and memories, representations and ideas, which form a kind of interior universe created by ourselves, in which we can be king and master, and which, even at a very early age, can be our dearest possession. She did not experience the need to know just for the sake of knowing, that is to say, for the sake of self-enrichment, or in order to obtain a certain security, to provide a refuge or consolation for oneself. Mary's love kept her always and in every way poor in spirit, never appropriating anything. It was a spontaneous tendency, resulting from the very impulse of her love, not to store up knowledge in her mind jealously like a treasure, but to give everything to her God.

She was also free from the excessive curiosity of an impatient reason that is not content with love alone; her attitude was one of a simple faith that trusted in the word of those she loved. The starting point for the development of her senses, imagination and reason was not curiosity, but a simple hunger for truth wholly inspired and enveloped by her faith. She had the faith of an infant, marked by trust and self-surrender. She sought for nothing on her own, but looked to her Heavenly Father for everything, and received everything with humility and gratitude.

The activity of Mary's mind and all her faculties was inspired directly by love, and was converted totally into thanksgiving, praise and adoration. This is why we say that she did not regard any knowledge as a property or possession. In her, there was not a *subject* attributing everything to itself; by her love, she was nothing but a relationship with her God. She was always a handmaiden, and a *poor* handmaiden at that.

At the beginning of her life, as we have seen, her charity had the simplest possible form, completely devoid of every accessory. The infant's natural love presupposes nothing more than that vital touch by which it is aware of its actual and almost substantial union with its mother. This, however, is ideally suited to the recipient of Infinite Love. Being destitute of knowledge and images made Mary utterly passive in regard to the Holy Spirit.

As Mary matured, her love developed rapidly and continuously, but did not grow *rich*; it simply entered more deeply into the bosom of the Heavenly Father, beyond all thought and representations, in the absolute of the union of love. What St. Thomas Aquinas discovered at the end of his life, and what St. John of the Cross teaches in the *Spiritual Canticle* — the summit of mystical knowledge, beyond which there lies nothing but the beatific vision — Mary possessed from the beginning, naturally as it were, and far more deeply and simply than these great mystics. She loved her God as the most tender and intimate of mothers, and it was this love which truly nourished her soul.

When she was old enough, this love impelled her to learn all she could about the Law and the prophets, the Word of God transmitted through the traditions of her people. With a faith full of humility and docility, and with loving attentiveness, she listened to her parents, the elders and the masters of the Law as they expounded all the teachings of tradition. With a faith that was pure, luminous and ardent, eager to know those friends of God who were her brothers and sisters in the faith, she learned about Abraham, Isaac, Jacob, Moses and all the prophets.

Love gave her a spontaneous understanding of the Scriptures, which she related to one another in the light of love. She would have done this particularly under the influence of the *Song of Songs* and of those prophets, such as Hosea, who had had the most tender and profound sense of the great mystery of God revealing himself to his people as the Beloved. By the inspiration of love, Mary had, even as an infant, a sense of union with God far more profound than that of the greatest metaphysicians or theologians. It was not so erudite, of course, but for that very reason was *truer* to the ineffable divine reality. It helped her to understand the figures of the prophets and the meaning of the story of creation. By the inner light of the Holy Spirit, the two orders of divine revelation — that of creation and that of the inspired Word — were united so as to complement each other, thereby preparing Mary for a third revelation which was to complete them — that of the Incarnate Word himself.

But the love which illumined and inspired her faith and made her attentive to her teachers, also detached her from all these figures and narratives, and even from the lights given to her. Her love for God was too intense and deep to allow her mind and imagination to adhere to mere symbols and suggestions. The God whom she knew intimately without any concept or representation always appeared infinitely more lovable and mysterious than any of these things. The words of the prophets, although received with a completely loving faith because they were the very words of her God, were nevertheless unable to satisfy her love with the substantial food for which she longed. Even though, as Queen of the Prophets, Mary grasped the sense of the prophecies far more profoundly than the doctors of the Law or even the prophets themselves, her faith endured a kind of poverty in contrast with theirs. Of all the disciples of her God, she was the most destitute and hence also the most eager.

We can see this even more concretely if we recall that Mary's grace was proportionate to her motherhood and adapted to it. Already from birth she had the grace of one who was to be the Mother of the Lord; even her initial love had something maternal about it. This inclined her to receive gratefully every word foretelling the Messiah, since she was drawn toward him with a kind of motherly affection. But at the same time this love detached her from the human materials that served as a vehicle for these revelations. Men affected by original sin, who live by their senses and imagination, need many explanations, comparisons and images. But the maternal heart of the Immaculate Virgin could not be satisfied with such illuminations; she needed, and her love gave her a sort of right to, the interior touch of the Holy Spirit. It was not in creation, nor in the history of mankind or of her people, even as known through the prophets, nor in the life she led in the community to which she belonged, that Mary spontaneously looked for God. The inherent drive of a love that was already maternal constantly withdrew her from all creatures and all the works of man to the silent, solitary intimacy with God which she found in her innermost depths.

Silence

After listening humbly and devoutly to the words of the prophets, and reciting the psalms and hymns of the Old Testament in fraternal union with her people, Mary longed to withdraw to a quiet place, where she could rest in silent prayer and daily plunge more deeply into the silence of love, which alone was able to assuage the burning ardors of her heart. For her, even more than for St. John of the Cross, silence was the language of God. Silence and poverty of spirit were intimately united in her life. No human word, not even one inspired by God, could satisfy the profound intention of love that oriented her faith. Without explicitly realizing it, her motherly love thirsted for a substantial word, for the Eternal Word himself. So long as he was not given to her, silence was the spontaneous and natural attitude of her soul.

In her humility, Mary undoubtedly sensed that the substantial light for which her love longed was not to be had in the darkness of faith. But in that silence which was the only true fullness she knew, the Holy Spirit must have given her some presentiment that God in his transcendence is able to find means other than human language to reveal himself to his people and to signify his love for them.

Silence brought Mary back to the simplicity of her first love for the God who did not yet speak to her as a teacher, nor even as a father, but nourished her as a mother, thereby suffusing her whole being with his love. In this silence, the Holy Spirit may even have given her the presentiment (not of course articulated) that this poor matter of which our bodies are made, precisely because of its utter indetermination and total passivity, has a much greater kinship with the infinity of Divine Love than do the ideas and images with which the human mind tries to grasp it.

In this silence, which kept Mary always at the source of her supernatural life and constantly disclosed new depths to her, the Holy Spirit prepared her for the great trial of faith which was to take place at the Annunciation. In this first phase of her life, in which her faith was nourished and enlightened through the doctrines of the Jewish tradition imparted by her teachers, Mary Queen of the Old and the New Testaments, relived Salvation History for her people, making reparation by her love for their infidelities and negligence.

At the same time, she experienced the illuminative way traveled by spiritual men and women of all times and places. However, it was above all in littleness and poverty that Mary's faith grew, because of the fullness of her love. In her, the unitive way preceded the illuminative. For our sakes, God led her through the development and growth involved in the instruction of faith which is characteristic of the illuminative way; but all the while she remained in the unitive way by her love. Even as it grew better informed and more explicit, traversing the thousands of years which separated her from Abraham, and from the beginnings of the human race, Mary's faith always retained the attitude of an infant.

In learning from the Holy Spirit, Mary was not conscious of history in the way we are as we journey through a time and space constructed by our reason in the memory and imagination. She grew aware of history in an infinitely more divine and more realistic way, by remaining in the poverty of the present moment, and in the silence required for that. The Holy Spirit, and he alone, imparts this silence of love, by uniting a person with Eternal Love. Thus he causes us to know temporal things according to God's good pleasure, keeping us detached from space and time. In this way too, the Immaculate Virgin maintained a poverty of spirit.

Humility and Docility

The second characteristic of Mary's spiritual life consisted in this, that the love dwelling in her made her naturally humble and gentle. She did not feel the need to dominate, to impose herself on others, to affirm herself through words, gestures and actions. This need, which appears early in the life of other children, reveals the birth of the aggressive ego, bent on breaking free from the yoke of love.

In the Book of Genesis, the murder of Abel by his brother Cain appears as the first consequence of original sin. Many psychologists are convinced that the deepest drive of the ego is that of aggression. The child loses the total, blind trust in love, and in the passivity required by love, which he had at the beginning. He wants to overcome obstacles by his own powers. He wants to experiment with and know for himself the new vital forces that he feels rising within him. Thus he acquires a taste for independence.

The need to dominate, which springs from an instinct of self-defense as well as from consciousness of one's vital energy, is much deeper in us than the need for immediate pleasure. It seems to be the mainspring of our psychology (at least since the fall) and of that hope in life which impels us spontaneously to act, expand, grow and progress. It is at the base of the myth of progress. This aggressive ego combines with the possessive ego to form the fundamental egotism that is so deep in us it seems natural. It is relatively easy to recognize that the quest of pleasure for pleasure's sake is a fault. The superficial egotism involved in it is quite evident. But we regard as natural, and almost virtuous, those deeper and utterly self-centered tendencies of the ego which form the basis of a personality unredeemed by grace.

Of course they have to be taken into consideration; and so long as the Holy Spirit has not purified us profoundly by making love the immediate and all-embracing mainspring of our life, we are wise in being content to moderate these self-centered drives, giving them the right mode and measure by employing them for the authentic goals of life. Only the graces of the unitive way can make us realize that these fundamental drives are not really natural, but are linked to an ego that has arisen subsequently and in opposition to love. There is in us something much deeper yet — a life force, or rather capacity, that is properly a capacity for love.

Mary, being sinless, did not have this ego which desires growth for its own sake, and which regards progress in all forms as an end in itself. On the contrary, she was drawn naturally toward littleness and humility. She was happy to remain dependent on God and obedient to him. She loved to trust him in everything, and to remain passive under the impulses that came from him. She never sought the first place, but was glad to efface herself before others. The beatitude of the meek and humble was fully realized in her, just like the beatitude of the poor in spirit. In her we can see the intimate connection between littleness and love; conversely, she helps us discern the selfish ego lurking in the desire of greatness for its own sake. All her life Mary remained an infant before her God, happy to look to him for everything and let herself be carried in his arms like a baby, relying on him in blind trust and total self-surrender. She never sought the independence of a will that wants to act on its own — an attitude incompatible with the dependence essential to true love. Never for an instant did she withdraw from the loving passivity demanded by the union of love. The deep interior attitude inspiring her entire life involved an awareness that love is a gift of God, one that is always in the act of being given, and which therefore requires that we remain in the actual embrace of the Holy Spirit, completely enfolded by his love.

The supernatural virtue of love or charity, infused into the soul by the Holy Spirit, passes through phases which are quite diverse: first, it furnishes the root motivation for voluntary activities that continue to be directed by reason in the normal manner of human acts; secondly, it produces affections of the heart which still belong to the realm of human psychology, but are inspired and actualized by the Holy Spirit's gift of wisdom; finally, it becomes a union of love that is direct and all-embracing, transforming our deepest psychology.

But this union of love, brought about by the fullest operation of the gift of wisdom, is too divine to be given to us as a permanent disposition or a kind of knowledge. Neither can it be given in the manner of a 'breath' or inspiration; for an inspiration, even though it requires that we remain more or less profoundly under its influence, does not demand the total surrender of our being. The union of love implies that all of our faculties are taken possession of by God. Hence it requires that we be totally surrendered to him, completely embraced by his love. The affectionate child stays within sight of his mother, responsive to her least gesture and most gentle suggestion. In this he differs from the adolescent, who is usually at some distance from her. But even the child's activities are his own; only the infant carried and nursed by its mother is able, through this intimate and vital contact, to know the union of love in its immediacy and totality.

The mystics say that the soul that is led along the path of love is immersed in God as in an ocean; it is carried by him, ravished by him, and drawn out of itself. It does not just receive the radiance and breath of God; God himself comes to it in person in the invisible mission of the Holy Spirit. He takes possession of the soul and carries it off, that it may abide in his love.

In Mary, and in her alone, divine charity took the form of this union of love totally and immediately, from the very first instant of her life. Of course she had to act too; all the activities normal to human life had a place in her life. But they were not merely *under the command of* charity nor even merely *inspired by* it, but *wholly infused with it* and *totally in its embrace.* The active mode of behavior characteristic of the ego was not there. Even in their execution, Mary's actions always remained under the influence of the loving passivity proper to the union of love. They were enveloped and interiorized by it. Exteriorly, they appeared like the actions of other human beings; but their motivation and inner psychology were radically different.

Similarly, Mary's life was inspired by a single hope, which sprang from love and had the form of trust and self-surrender. She did not have that self-confidence which is part and parcel of the ego. All the growth in her life took place under the sign of a hope inspired by love, constantly looking to her Father for everything. She acted indeed, but always in the embrace of the Spirit, "leaning up on her beloved," who was God himself. In the truest sense of the words, Mary had no desires of her own, but only desires inspired by love, desires which served to express this love.

We might then be inclined to suppose that she was above all a soul of desire; but no, more than anything else, hers was a *soul of thanksgiving*. The *Magnificat* expresses the fundamental attitude of the humble and magnanimous handmaid of the Lord. At each step of her life, the Holy Spirit overwhelmed his bride in a measure far surpassing all her desires, even her possible desires. In Mary, grace was always prior to nature; and, as her soul mounted upwards, the impulse of the Holy Spirit always exceeded the measure of grace actually present in her, thus keeping her in an attitude of thanksgiving that grew constantly more intense.

On the other hand, Mary's love gave her such a sense of the mystery in which she was involved, and such humility, that she did not presume to undertake anything on her own initiative. She felt unable to express in definite desires that which the Holy Spirit made her sense in the silence of love. Any specific and formulated request would have been inferior to the gift for which the Holy Spirit was preparing her. This is why her deepest prayer, the one most proper to her and best suited to her soul, was a loving silence in which gratitude and petition were joined. By it she allowed the Holy Spirit himself to desire in and through her. Thereby he was able to manifest to her his least will whenever he saw fit.

CHAPTER 3

Mary's Virginal Love

Now we must seek to discover the third characteristic of Mary's Immaculate Heart — one which will disclose to us the secret of her soul. Instead of a pleasure-seeking ego, she had a love that was essentially virginal. But we must take care to understand in what sense this was so, and how this virginal love enveloped Mary's entire body, her physical life and all her activities.

Whereas in English we give Mary the title of *Blessed Virgin*, in French she is more often called the 'Holy Virgin.' She is the holy one in whom everything is virginal; the virgin in whom everything is holy. Her love was essentially virginal because it always drew her back into the most profound interior of her soul, into the inmost recess of consciousness, thus preserving her from ever seeking pleasure simply for its own sake. Mary did not focus on any pleasure in itself. What was said above about her knowledge applies also to her joys: they always arose from love. They were inspired by love and in turn fostered it; they sprang from it and terminated in it. They never broke out of the sphere of love to take on a consistency of their own through a reflex movement of the ego turning back upon self.

Mary surely had a sense of the beautiful to an eminent degree. She must have had a sense for the beauties of nature as well as those of Sacred Scripture. But in her this sense was very different from what it is in us, because it originated directly in love and terminated, not in a representation of the beautiful object, but in a genuine love for it. Thus she was aware of earth's beauties in and by love, and she loved them in accordance with the way they had been disposed by God.

In the case of things or animals, are they not, in the art of God's love, chiefly reflections and signs which speak to us of his love, but which do not have a proper value in and by themselves? Mary saw them, heard them and appreciated them with a sensitivity more refined than that of any artist. Her understanding, immersed in love, was aware of their value as signs; but her heart did not repose in these faint traces of the divine, it reposed simply in the love which they signified.

Reason (not the same thing as understanding) works quite differently: it is forever seeking to analyze objects and to form representations of them. It undertakes to complete that which, in the plans of God, is meant to be transitory and unfinished. For God has left some things unstable and hence imperfect precisely so that they will not hold our attention, but only arouse it and direct it elsewhere.

In persons, on the contrary (especially those in greatest misery), Mary's love recognized not only *traces* of God but real *images* created in his likeness. They do have a proper value in themselves. In them, in their substance, Mary's love encountered her God. No doubt, these images are in themselves quite imperfect; they are mainly possibilities and capacities of love. But the Holy Spirit caused Mary to know them in his love and in accordance with his loving plans for them for this very reason that, through her love, she might fulfill their capacities and complete their barely sketched resemblances.

Incidentally, we can see here again the profound connection between silence and virginal love. The ego detests silence. It is always on the go and agitated. Its existence is bound up with the imagination and the desires arising therefrom, which are incompatible with both silence and rest. Noisy by nature, the ego lives on comparisons, contrasts, conflicts and compromise. As a result, it can never create a lasting unity. Its transitory compositions tend toward dissolution because of the very elements that compose them, and they are called into question by every new factor coming into the picture. For the imagination is set in motion, both by the cupidities inherent in the ego, and by everything that strikes the external senses. There is nothing in the imagination that can impart a genuine unity to what it receives.

Source of Her Inner Life

Psychologically and subjectively speaking, that which is deepest in our psychic life is the subconscious, formed long before rational consciousness. Being the result of all the drives of our ego, it is more like a stagnant well — but one that is bottomless, since the imagination is essentially indefinite. In Mary, on the contrary, the deepest root and constant nourishment of her inner life was a love that was like a virginal spring. It was not contaminated by any foreign element; rather, whatever it touched, with the touch of love, it purified, by uniting it with God. This consciousness was by its very essence a source of unity.

Mary's virginal love made her go beyond all the thoughts, images, and lights of her mind. Even though these were all completely translucent to her inner light, and were even like reflections of that mysterious light which is love, they were not substantial enough to serve as the instrument or direct matter of the union of love. Consequently, this virginal love drew Mary back constantly into the inmost recesses of her being, where it had first been given to her. This love was jealous in its virginity; it kept her reason and imagination prisoners.

On the other hand, it pervaded her entire body. From deep within her, it seemed to pour itself out like an ointment, enveloping her completely. It held her in a gentle but powerful immobility, imparting a kind of rest, refreshment and warmth. Mary's love communicated a kind of virginity, not only to her mind, but even to her senses, internal as well as external. For her, anything that would withdraw a person from love, anything that attached the heart to a creature, anything that remained simply exterior to love, was an impurity. It may have been the most luminous of aesthetic perceptions, but it could have no part in her interior life.

Love made Mary live in the God in whom nothing is alien to love. In God, knowledge itself is at the same time love. So likewise for the Bride of the Holy Spirit: all her relationships, both with people and with things, existed under the sign of love.

The interior universe in which Mary lived, poor, humble and silent under the inspiration of the Holy Spirit, was very different from the inner world constructed by our imagination and ego. Our inner world is still 'the world.' Whether it be the world of the artist, the painter or even of the 'natural mystic,' it remains essentially a quantitative world, in which some form of greatness is what counts. It is a world that looks for endless progress in time and extension in space. In it, even persons are represented and conceived according to external appearances.

The universe which Mary carried in her heart was hidden even from herself. Only the Holy Spirit could reveal it to her when he so pleased, and only for the actual moment. This interior universe did not consist of objects and images, but of persons. The people she knew and loved were what defined and shaped the world for her. All the images by which the things we know are represented in our minds, and all the relationships between subject and object, the knowing person and the thing known, were in her case totally assimilated and so to speak dissolved into the interpersonal relations of love inspired by the Holy Spirit.

The egotism that is found in all of us compels us to acknowledge the depth and extent of the Blessed Virgin's holiness. Through their mystical knowledge the saints realize that the ego leaves its mark on all our psychic activities because of the affective link (often quite unconscious) these have with the ego. Modern psychology confirms these affirmations of the saints (which philosophers often used to regard as exaggerated) by drawing attention to the deep-seated tendency of the subject to view every object in relation to itself. This unconscious tendency, which takes shapes long before the awakening of conscience, lies at the origin of all our activities, although one may be quite unaware of it. Its effect is that we do not encounter the world with an objective or indifferent attitude, but with the self-centeredness of a subject which instinctively relates everything to itself.

Mary, on the contrary, was not a subject whose consciousness consisted in an existence in and for herself; she was a *conscious person*, whose very existence consisted in a love relationship with God. In the deepest core of her inner life, she was a bride wholly turned toward the Divine Spouse and subordinated to him. Her personality was constituted in and by this *esse ad* — this "being for another" — of an existentialism of love. While eliminating the foundation and even the very subject of philosophical existentialism, this existentialism of love provides the only adequate response to the questions raised by the former, and to the obscure presentiments which give existentialism the fragments of truth which make it so seductive.

Root of Her Poverty and Humility

Poverty of spirit, humility of heart and virginity are thus the characteristic notes of the interior of Mary's soul, in which there was no room for an ego. We can go one step further and say that virginal love inspired the other two, and therefore most properly constituted her interior — that deep inner consciousness which, instead of inclining her toward external grandeur, as does the ego, drew her inward, toward intimacy and littleness.

Poverty and humility are the attitudes of creatures, and even more precisely of 'wayfarers' — those who have not yet a fixed abode in the Blessed Trinity. They are the two most basic attitudes of the created intellect and will confronted with a God who deigns to reveal the mystery of his being in faith and hope. Faith implies detachment from light, and therefore poverty; hope implies the absolute confidence and total self-surrender of a child that looks to its Heavenly Father for everything, hence humility. Only love can bring about such an utter stripping of the spirit. Love likewise imparts its own mode to faith and hope, enabling them to remain interior to love even while exercising their own specific function.

Divine Source of Virginal Love

The virginity of love is nothing other than its interiority. This quality comes directly from Infinite Love itself, and keeps the mark of its origin. The love of the three Persons of the Blessed Trinity for one another cannot, strictly speaking, be called *poor* or *humble* (although it can be so called in a 'virtual' sense). Even though we are made like the Divine Persons by poverty and humility, and unlike them by the proprietorship and independence of the ego, one cannot rightly speak of poverty or humility in the relationships of the Divine Persons with one another.

But the love which creates the utterly interior and intimate union of the Divine Persons does have a truly *virginal* character. The mystery of the Blessed Trinity involves a union, or rather unity, in which there is no exteriority or division whatsoever. The three Persons are all interior to one another. The Father engenders a Son who abides "in his bosom" (according to the literal sense of John 1:18). This generation does not entail any separation; it takes place in perfect unity. Similarly, in the 'spiration' of love, Father and Son give their entire substance to the Holy Spirit, who in turn remains interior to them as the personal gift of each to the other.

Mary did not become expressly aware of this mystery of Infinite Love until the Annunciation, when it was revealed to her very concretely through the Incarnation. Nevertheless, her virginal love had already given her an obscure presentiment of it. When she was a child, God did not reveal himself to her as the Transcendent, or the extrinsic Last End, but as the *God of love*, interior to her soul. She was well aware that the Spirit of God condescended to live within her, and to unite himself with her in a real union of love. He was not merely the breath which animated all creation and inspired the prophets; this breath came to abide as a person, a beloved person, in this, the least of his creatures. He was therefore Love in person.

In and by this love, God appeared to her as a father giving life to his child, as a beloved father, as a friend in the profoundest sense, who himself lived the same life he gave to her. Yet Mary was so deeply aware that love, as an absolutely free gift of God, transcends all created life, even requiring the sacrifice of light and life, that she did not know whether there is life, strictly speaking, in God. All she knew was that God was not only Infinite Goodness, attracting her as an end that is extrinsic and remote; he was also Love, giving himself to her in person.

For her, God was above all the unique, Infinite Love that gave himself to her without any external sign. He was an infinite, virgin spring deep within her, attracting her. She felt drawn to him, she lost herself in him. This spring was like an entire universe — a dimensionless universe — in which she found herself in a new love relationship with all those persons with whom God had united her.

In the Trinity, the relationships of love create a true unity between persons such as can never exist, with the same degree of realism, outside of supernatural love. Mary was well aware that the love relationship which she experienced had an immediacy, totality and actuality altogether different from the intentionality of knowledge, or of a merely affective union.[6] But she had no way of knowing, during this first period of her life, whether there could be actual relationships within the very mystery of God.

Virginal Love and Mary's Physical Life

We have already noted that Mary's virginal love radiated upon her entire body and physical life, infusing into them a luminous, interior purity, and giving a special significance to her vow of virginity.

In us, temperance, which is the last of the four cardinal virtues, is an essentially particular virtue by reason of its matter and form. The matter with which it is properly concerned consists of the pleasures of touch.[7] Temperance does not bear directly on the vital activities of eating, drinking and sex, but attains them only through the intermediary of the sensible pleasures that accompany them. Consequently, temperance is unable to purify our vital activities in their root and source. It must be content to give them their due measure, to moderate them 'reasonably,' so that the ego, in its eagerness for pleasure, will not use them to the detriment of the deep purposes of human life, or in contradiction to the law of God.

Mary's virginal love, however, was not thus limited. On the contrary, it took hold of all the capacities and energies of her human life, even the deepest and most hidden, at their inner source. It sanctified and unified them interiorly by attracting them and uniting them to God. To begin with, it sanctified the infant Mary's vital relations

42

with her mother, St. Ann, turning them into a kind of natural sacrament of divine love. We have already seen how the very first love inspiring these relationships in Mary was supernaturalized; now we must try to glimpse the consequences of this fact in the development of her physical life.

The artist who tries to grasp the deep and hidden significance of human realities cannot look upon the nursing of a baby by its mother as a purely physical function, pertaining solely to the 'vegetative' life. This activity, especially on the part of the infant, involves something very pure, spiritual and even mysterious. As a result of original sin, the mother too often fails to realize fully the deep significance and far-reaching implications of this activity for her child; but the attitude of the latter has a kind of religious and recollected quality. This is so, regardless of its family background.

In analyzing such things, the adult is always in danger of misinterpreting them in function of his own feelings and emotions, which may not yet exist in the baby. A simple and pure soul, however, does not make this mistake. It senses in this act a depth and intimacy, the meaning of which it is not able to grasp fully. The remarks of simple people often show that this scene makes them think almost spontaneously of the infant Jesus. (Only at this early age, and in these intimate relationships with its mother, does the child retain fully its natural resemblance to Jesus.)

To reduce nursing to a mere nutritional function is to see only its material aspect. The echo of mystery in it, its purity and spirituality, come from the fact that, at a deeper and more vital level, it is a wholly pure union of love between two conscious human persons. This is especially the case on the part of the infant. Its attitude is completely different from that of an animal, and contrasts even with that of its older brother who, in eating his porridge, has grown independent of his mother. The willful and greedy ego manifested by the latter highlights, by contrast, the simplicity and mysterious depth of the infant. However, the infant's love is merely natural, unconscious and feeble. Only by recourse (in prayer) to the mystery of Jesus as an infant nursing at the breast can we sense the deep meaning that this primordial activity must have had in Mary's own life. It was already a kind of preparation for her divine maternity.

Mary never lost this initial love. Throughout her life, in eating and drinking, as in all her physical comportment, she retained the simplicity of the infant. Her love regarded the food she ate as taken from the fruit and the harvest that had been prepared carefully by the Heavenly Father himself for his little daughter. Her daily bread came from him. (The poor in spirit and humble of heart have this privilege of realizing that they are nourished by their God.)

Mary's food was simple, taken directly from nature and retaining the characteristics given it by nature. It did not have the banality and vulgarity of our manufactured and stockpiled commodities. What is more, Mary did not treat it with the indifference — one might almost say brutality — of those imbued with the spirit of the machine age. She looked upon the things she ate as a nourishment animated by the breath of life that comes directly from God. In them, her love discovered a taste and a fragrance of God, put there by the Spirit to remind us of his love which created everything for human beings and for their union with him.

In her relationships with nature, Mary already conducted herself as queen of the universe, conscious that the King of Kings, with his art of love, had arranged everything, down to the least details, for this little child of his predilection. She sensed that the art of love does not create things in series. It is the individual reality, in that singleness of its existence which alone can be loved directly, that bears the imprint of Infinite Love. In the countless little touches which analytical reason ascribes to change and contingency, Mary's loving heart recognized signs of the gratuity, liberty and utterly disinterested generosity of the love of her God.

The art of divine love is not a 'plastic' art, like sculpture or painting, which produces inert objects that are purely representational; it is more like a musical word (e.g., a song in praise of God) or like the Word of God itself, which is kept in existence by the actual breath of God, who gives it at each instant whatever note he pleases. Creation itself is a Word of God, thanks to the light which suffuses it — a light that is mixed with darkness. (It is the role of the prophets to give us the exact sense of this word, as well as to proclaim the One who gives the universe its ultimate explanation.)

Virginal Love and the Mystery of Matter

Mary must have sensed that, besides the mystery of God as Infinite Love, there is another mystery in the matter of which this world is formed. Its infinite capacity utterly eludes the created intellect. Its impenetrable darkness makes it too in some way an object of faith. It is bound up with the *realism* of the mystery of faith, of which Mary was deeply conscious. On the other hand, precisely because of this darkness and all that it entails, matter also implies a mystery of humility and passivity in regard to Infinite Love: matter is permeable and malleable to love in a way that reason and imagination can never be.

The very poverty of matter gives it a kind of affinity with Infinite Love: the affinity of the infinitely little with the infinitely great. Because of its poverty, matter offers a capacity which, although created, is potentially infinite. Matter is something pure and virginal, in which Love can reveal itself. This it does in the form of humble traces pertaining to the sense of touch. The latter may be the poorest of all the senses at determining the qualities of things, but it is the one that attains most nearly to their substance. For it is as breath, spirit, respiration, living water, refreshment, warmth, anointing and fire that Infinite Love presents itself to us. Mary sensed that this boundless capacity of matter had been created directly and properly by Infinite Love so that the entire universe might be kept permanently and totally in the grasp of love and, above all, available for the union of love.

Love must have given Mary an obscure sense of the distinction between *prime matter*,[8] which totally eludes the efforts of human reason to grasp it, and seems to be a domain that God reserves to himself, and *quantified mat-*

ter — the intelligible, rational matter with which created intelligence works. The latter is the principle of division, of exteriority, contrariety and mobility. The former is a capacity of unity and penetrability in which Mary perceived a mysterious affinity with her virginal love. The latter, which the intellect abstracts from reality and from the real measures given by God, is a kind of accomplice of the ego. It is the proper domain of that falsely interior world created by and for the appetites of the ego.

This subtle distinction has been attained with great difficulty by theologians grappling with the mysteries of the Eucharist and the Incarnation. Not metaphysical reasoning but love made Mary aware of this distinction naturally and experientially, as it were, even before the birth of Jesus. Two factors led her to it: her intimate union with God, and in him with all the persons to whom he united her; and her acute sense of poverty and of the present instant, which demanded total detachment from imagination and memory, as well as from time and space.

CHAPTER 4

Mary, the First Consecrated Virgin

We have seen that Mary's interior life was constituted primarily by her virginal love, which is like a spring of living water rising out of the depths of her soul under the action of the Holy Spirit. Now we must examine what may be called her religious life. The Presentation in the Temple and the vow of virginity associated with her marriage to Joseph gave Mary's life a profound resemblance to that of professed religious today.

Mary's Consecration to God

Mary was the first person to live according to the evangelical counsels.[9] She inaugurated this new form of life even before Jesus himself gave the example and recommendation of it. Being immaculate, she had no need of an ascetical life in the strict sense. It was not for the sake of conversion that she chose a life of total sacrifice in poverty, humility and obedience. Rather, divine love itself impelled her to withdraw from the world and shun its spirit of hunger for wealth, power and pleasure. She did not fear any complicity with it, but she wanted to avoid its complications and bondages as much as possible, so that love might be completely free to grow and develop in her.

Jesus had the beatific vision, which actualized and stabilized his love at a maximum which nothing could diminish or obscure. Mary, however, lived under the regime of faith and her charity had to be exercised and developed in darkness. Even though, at the deepest level, her life was constantly oriented toward God, her charity (like ours) was at any given moment actualized more or less totally, depending on external circumstances and still more on her inner dispositions. It was subject to the fundamental weakness of all love in this world — that of being affected by the conditions of its milieu. The extreme intensity of Mary's love, in a mind and body which retained their natural weakness, made it vitally necessary for her to keep all the attention of her mind and all the energy of her heart focused exclusively on God. In order to discern his will fully and freely, she needed to be recollected.

Mary's faith, fully illumined by the Holy Spirit, perceived traces of Infinite Love — of its gentleness, strength and tender solicitude, in everything. But a trace is only a sign barely indicated, and the very purpose of the traces of the divine in nature is to prevent us from stopping at creatures. They refer us beyond the created order to where we may, in silence and solitude, discover the full substance and truth of the divine mystery. The gifts of the Holy Spirit do not make us see things bathed in the light of glory. They do not give us a kind of supernatural aesthetic appreciation. Rather they make us sense an obscure reflection of love in a mixture of light and darkness. The light by which they see comes from a hidden source, and draws us away from the creature to find this source deep within ourselves, in the night of faith.

Mary's living faith made her take ceaseless care not to allow visible things or external circumstances to distract her from the one thing necessary — the Eternal, which here on earth is hidden and invisible. Above all, Mary had to live by faith and love amid a world of sin and sinners, in a society of structures, institutions and laws, the spirit of which was hostile to the aspirations awakened in her by the Holy Spirit.

An ancient tradition has it that when she was old enough to act on her own, and choose the kind of life best suited to the interior call she felt so strongly, Mary decided (with the help of the Holy Spirit, who already dwelt in her in all his fullness) to leave her parents' home, her family and the society of her close friends, and go to the Temple to consecrate herself completely to God. She was, however, still very young, just a child. This belief has come down to us in the feast of Mary's Presentation in the Temple. Modern historical studies indicate that the origin of this tradition is legendary; nevertheless, this popular belief impresses an accurate recognition of the totality of Mary's devotedness to God.[10]

The mystery of the Presentation is completed by that of

Mary's vow of virginity and marriage with St. Joseph. These two mysteries situate Mary in the religious state even before the birth of Jesus. Because of them, she may be regarded as the hidden foundress of the religious life, just as she is its Queen and Mother.

These two mysteries are the only ones in which Mary took a properly personal initiative in regard to her external activities, acting as master of her own destiny, as an adult capable of self-determination. And she used this power only to relinquish the independence it might have conferred on her. She deliberately chose a state of life that was radically new by comparison with the Old Testament and the religious history of mankind. Under the inspiration of the Holy Spirit, she and Joseph together inaugurated a state of *royal servitude* and *spiritual childhood*. These mysteries define an economy or regimen in which we can admire both the wisdom of the Holy Spirit and the humility and magnanimity of Mary and Joseph.

Humility

Mary did not withdraw into the desert as John the Baptist was later to do. The Holy Spirit inspired her to adopt a way of life similar in external appearance to that of everyone else. By choosing a state sanctioned by custom and recognized by law, one that attracted no special attention to herself, she was able to remain hidden from the eyes of the world and even from those of her own family.

Like any girl of her age, Mary entered into marriage. But Joseph was the 'confidant' of the aspirations inspired in her by the Holy Spirit. Joseph himself had been prepared by the Spirit of God for his unique vocation. He was the "just man" (Matthew 1:19), who sought nothing other than the will of God, who already hungered and thirsted for God's justice. Like Mary, he was pained at the indifference of the great mass of his people, at their practical neglect of the prophetic promises and the messianic expectations, at their inordinate attachment to riches and pleasure, at their servility, so ready to surrender independence in faith and religion in order to obtain the earthly advantages and moral license which came with the Roman domination.

Like Mary, Joseph had a pure heart. He detested the hypocrisy and legalism of the scribes and pharisees. In all things, he sought only to please God, without concern for the esteem or reproof of others. Like Mary, he was a person of discretion and silence in regard to the secrets of God. Even before the coming of Jesus, he sensed that the mystery of faith could develop only in our innermost depths. Like the greatest mystics, he must have been aware already that no human word is suitable to express the most divine working of the Spirit of God which takes place in the silence of love. This silence made him the faithful and prudent servant, able to become the guardian of the Bride of the Holy Spirit. Joseph's silence arose from his humility; but this humility, born of love, was completely magnanimous. It was capable of understanding and espousing Mary's own queenly magnanimity.

Magnanimity

For Aristotle and the men of antiquity, magnanimity was the virtue that kept a person from getting caught in the many different preoccupations, desires, joys and sufferings of the ordinary man. Most people have an active and, in fact, agitated psychology, because they stay immersed in the complexity and incessant changes of external things. The magnanimous mind, on the contrary, can discern in all this multiplicity that which is essential and has value in itself. Only the true finalities of life, which orient us toward our last end, interest him and retain his attention. Hence he is able to lead others, because his mind, will and heart remain constantly directed toward the goal by an intention that is always actual.

Mary's magnanimity was that of a queen — the queen of the universe — a queen of love who knew the King of Kings, and by her love lived continuously in the intimacy of his presence. No external event distracted her mind and heart from the interior presence of the Beloved, or separated her will from his least pleasure.

The magnanimous man of the ancients moved and spoke very little, because he was interested only in spiritual goods, which are few, as Aristotle observed. Mary kept silence; she never acted solely on her own impulse, because her love united her to the Subsistent Good itself, to the One Thing Necessary, to the very reality of the Last End dwelling within her in a presence that was both intimate and total.

The magnanimous man of the ancients was the guardian of tradition. He was the only one who had the keenness of vision and the courage to stand firm against the tide of popular opinion, and to go against the stream of his time without wearying. By being faithful to the true finalities of things (which derive from no other source than the divinity) he kept his people oriented toward the eternal.

As a girl, hardly more than a child, living in the darkness of faith, Mary relied solely on the interior call of the Spirit of God in order to be faithful to the spirit by which sacred tradition was animated. She broke with the customs of her people by the deliberate orientation she gave to her entire life. Together with Joseph, her confidant, support and spouse, she was the first to enter upon this entirely new way of life, and to consecrate herself exclusively to her God.

Thus Mary went forward alone, not concerned about the behavior of those who had gone before her, not wondering whether others would come after her, completely unaware that she would be followed along this royal path by Jesus himself and a multitude of brothers and sisters. She lived in the present moment, detached from the past and future, firmly fixed in this intention of the Holy Spirit that had been made manifest to her heart.

Who is this who comes alone up this narrow path (Song of Songs 3:6) to meet her beloved — a beloved as yet unknown to her, who had not yet appeared in the world, but existed only in his eternal nature with the Father? Without being aware of it, Mary anticipated him, even before his birth.

Mary's Vow of Virginity

In Mary and Joseph we find, in an eminent mode, the fundamental inclinations which are at the origin of all religious life. The poor, humble, virginal household in which they led this common life of silence corresponds to the three religious vows, as well as to the state of royal servitude and spiritual childhood which these vows call for. This household was like a visible sign of the profound harmony between the vows and Mary's most intimate aspirations.

We sinners do not have as the root of our religious life the virginal source of love that Mary had. Hence we need to express first the vow of obedience, which in a sense embraces the other two. The proper subject matter of the vow of obedience is indeed that which most hinders us from attaining the perfection of charity: namely the desire for independence in our aggressive, imperious ego. Hence this vow enables us to offer God the tremendous sacrifice of our right to control our external activities and life, the independence of action that is so dear to us.

We begin with a conversion, for we enter the religious state directly in order to engage in the purgative and illuminative life, and thus prepare ourselves for the unitive life if it pleases God to bestow this further gift. What we need above all is a stable assurance of the good use of our will. This is provided — insofar as it can be provided at all — by the vow of obedience, which puts our will under the direction of a prudent superior. The latter has above all the grace of state to direct the exterior activity of our new life. We could give no more authentic token of good will than this vow; for the will is the root from which all the activities of human life spring.

But Mary's life began, as we have seen, with the grace of the unitive way. This grace inspired and enveloped not only her external activities (which are in everyone directly submissive to the reason and will), but also the affections of her heart and even her physical energies. For her, the matter of obedience (as well as of poverty) was more restricted than that of virginity. The latter, in its concrete reality in her, embraced her entire being, which was formed into one, indivisible, substantial whole, by the virginal love which impregnated and enveloped it.

Mary's virginity was a true mystery. In the first place, it constituted the most intimate and interior aspect of her love. It gave her inner life its proper light and dynamics, or rather attraction. It extended outward, embracing her entire body, giving it an inner unity and making it a privileged matter and instrument of love. In giving her body to God, Mary gave him at the same time her will and all her affections besides. The entire substance of her being was given to God through her virginity.

Love impelled Mary to formulate explicitly the intention of remaining a virgin (Luke 1:34). This in turn embraced and inspired her poverty and obedience. These latter did not present any difficulty for her. She naturally sought a life that was simple and poor. She did not have a domineering ego, but spontaneously and lovingly obeyed the representative of God who had been provided to care for her exterior life, and thus exempt her from concern about subsistence or the management of the household. Joseph's guardianship made it possible for her to devote herself freely to the contemplative life. It enabled her to have the simplicity of an infant, who can remain silent and is not bound by a multitude of social relationships. Neither poverty nor obedience constituted for Mary the matter of a true sacrifice or holocaust.

By the vow of virginity, on the contrary, with the uniquely plenary meaning that it had in her case, her entire being and life were given to God as matter prepared for the sacrifice, so that the fire of heaven might descend and consume it. Her immaculate body was like a tiny privileged domain, which she offered to her God by her vow.

Mary's vow definitely and solemnly fulfilled the promise of total consecration which she had made to God at her 'Presentation.' At that time, Mary had been too young to have the proper matter of the vow of virginity; she had been in possession only of the rational, free faculty which permitted her to dispose of herself. Grace had impelled her to give what she did not yet possess, so as never to be proprietor of it even for an instant, and to be consecrated in advance by a state of voluntary poverty. When, as an adolescent, she became aware of the forces in her heart and body enabling her to establish a family of her own, and thus also was permitted to offer to God the proper matter of the vow of virginity, her consecration was complete, even though she still did not know the unique vocation God had reserved for her.

It is to be noted that Mary's vow of virginity was a consecration more than a promise. A promise has to do with something definite and limited. As a promise, Mary's vow had to be conditional and dependent on any new manifestation of God's will in the future, as St. Thomas points out.[11] Otherwise, there would not have been a true marriage between her and Joseph, to whom she had to surrender the right over her body.

The consecration, however, bore upon the total mystery of her body. It consisted simply in Mary's placing herself in the hands of God. Hence, the very uncertainty about how God was going to realize the sacrifice she offered was itself part of the sacrifice. Thus her consecration was absolutely definitive; she knew without any doubt that her body ought to be consecrated and reserved entirely for God to dispose of as he saw fit. Let us examine in more detail this first consecration of a Christian virgin.

Mary's Consecration

Two opposite types of inclination appear at the age of puberty in all of us who have been born with original sin; they may be called higher aspirations and lower instincts. There are noble, spiritual aspirations, springing from a deep affectivity within us, which in turn is inspired by that first natural love given us by God. The latter has not been obliterated by the ego but simply supplanted and driven underground (in greater or lesser measure) in our psychic life. Hence, at the age of puberty, youth experiences a desire to be of service and to live a life of generosity and disinterestedness. This appears along with concern for others and the desire to take one's place in society and to maintain the family traditions. Such aspirations give a spiritual significance to the differentiation of the sexes and their complementary roles.

On the one hand, a young man has a natural sense of respect for a girl, and in particular for her virginity. There is something religious about the attitude she inspires in him. He feels naturally inclined to be her defender and chivalrous servant. He senses a mystery in her very weakness and delicacy. She is the bearer of a secret and thereby appears to him, in a way that is difficult to articulate but deeply felt, as holy, as a kind of sign of the sacred. She is the one 'naturally' destined for the prayer of recollection and the role of intimate confidante of God. Men who keep an honest simplicity in their outlook sense an affinity between a girl's virginity and the religious life, especially the contemplative life. They have a spontaneous respect for the religious sister, and especially for the cloistered nun.

Reciprocally, a girl has a natural admiration for the clear-sighted, open countenance of a pure young man. The virility of his mind, and even his whole physical bearing, makes him appear to her as a sign of the strength and authority of God. Dare we say he is naturally destined to be her teacher, apostle and priest? (The strident discussion of 'feminist' issues in our day has made it very difficult to express such views serenely; but may it not be that the traditional conception of male and female roles embodies some authentic insights that may indeed need to be refined, but not indiscriminately suppressed by too crude an assault on sexism?)[12]

At the same time as these noble aspirations, the lower instincts of concupiscence also make a new appearance. They become much more active, aggressive and energetic than before. They find accomplices in the pleasure-loving, fantasizing ego. These lower drives, supported by the imagination and passions, contradict in every conceivable way the higher aspirations, which are weak by reason of their very delicacy. In their roots, these aspirations are pure, but they are easily contaminated, above all in a society which no longer maintains the traditions destined to support and explicate them. (In fact, today's society allows and actually fosters the development of the spirit of the world and its concupiscence. The delicate germs of chivalry and heroism are in danger of being stifled before they even begin to bud.)

In Mary and Joseph, the noble aspirations appeared at the age of adolescence as they do in others. But they were not tenuous and feeble, springing like passing breaths from a hidden, subconscious source. In Mary, in particular, there was no egocentric concupiscence to resist or tarnish them. Her physical powers developed under the inspiration of love and appeared to her consciousness not properly as vital energies or as drives aroused by exterior contacts and interior imaginations, but as new dispositions of love, totally at the disposal of her God. They remained under the ascendancy of his love, ready to be molded by his inspirations, oriented toward him and attracted by him.

The Marriage of Joseph and Mary

Mary's initial love had received instruction from the divine revelation handed down in the tradition of her people. The Scriptures recounted the creation of man and woman, domestic incidents in the lives of the patriarchs, the whole history of the Jews and the doctrine of the prophets. From this teaching, but always under the inspiration of love, Mary became aware of the distinct roles of man and woman in the home and in society. They are like two incomplete images of a single love, each of which helps the other draw nearer to God, and prepare for the loving union with God that is given in darkness and silence, with no figure or sign.

For Mary, Joseph was a representative of God, the image of divine authority ("The husband is head of the wife," Ephesians 5:23). By his prudence, his silence (which suggests also wisdom and magnanimity), and by his strength, Joseph was the guardian that God had prepared for her. Mary's virginal love kept her imagination and memory in a state of poverty, because it drew all her thoughts and recollections into her heart, and held her attention constantly in the present moment. This made her humanly very weak, so long as the Holy Spirit himself did not intervene to awaken the memories that lay dormant in her love. This poverty, which greatly fostered her contemplative life, was also willed by the Holy Spirit as a way to unite her all the more deeply to Joseph, who provided her with the services she needed. He was the intermediary between her and the world, the one accountable for her vis-à-vis the public authorities.

Joseph's previous sense of the mysterious sacredness of virginity was deepened and strengthened by his life with Mary. She was the bearer of a secret he was bound to respect and if necessary defend against the indiscreet or critical observations of others. He himself could benefit from it only in silence. He was happy to devote his strength and his labors to serve this delicate being whose weakness was accentuated by the passivity of her love.

Joseph was like an elder brother chosen and given to Mary directly by God. He was the 'neighbor' in the Christian sense, whom she in turn could help by those services which her very love wanted to render. Marriage gave her a companion in a shared life, enabling her to associate her contemplation with a constant exercise of fraternal charity — one that harmonized with her contemplation and prolonged it.

Marriage constituted Mary and Joseph as a household officially recognized by the authorities of the messianic people. So far as the external and fraternal life of this household is concerned, Joseph was the visible representative of God for Mary. Even more, he was the one designated for her by the Holy Spirit. He had the prophetic grace to direct this 'first monastery.' In this perspective, he appears as the last and best prefiguration of Jesus, one formed by the Holy Spirit for Mary alone.

Joseph's loyalty to Mary had a supernatural character. He knew that the Spirit of God lived in her and he trusted her completely. In his house, she was even freer than she had been in her parents' home to follow the heavenly inspirations. He was aware of her secret vow, and had accepted it as part of the marriage covenant by which they were united in the eyes of Hebrew society. He regarded himself primarily as her protector and guardian. He was ready to use his authority as a shelter in the human world for the work that God wished to accomplish in her.

It was Joseph's silence which drew Mary to him. What truly united their hearts was this common love of silence given them by the Holy Spirit. Their affection for each other was properly supernatural. The Holy Spirit himself had inspired their choice of each other: he was the unique beloved who united them.

The love of Mary and Joseph for each other was not a pleasure-seeking love. They were indeed a source of joy for each other; but pleasure was not their aim. This applies not only to carnal pleasure, but even to the spiritual delight in conversation and sharing which foster a reciprocal cognizance of one another's thoughts and sentiments. Their love was plunged in silence. It is often said that the friend of God finds his joy in the God of grace, not in the grace of God. Similarly, when the Holy Spirit unites his friends to one another, it is not in order to enrich them, even spiritually, by their mutual regard; it is in order that they might help one another become purified of egotism and plunged into the silence of love.

The union between Mary and Joseph was immeasurably more profound, intimate and delicate than any other human affection; but it was also situated on quite a different plane. It was born in silence, consummated in silence and sealed by silence. Thus it remained completely virginal. At the deepest level, virginity of heart and interior silence coincide in divesting us of all those mutual exchanges which constitute our spiritual wealth.

Mary and Joseph were united in order to lead together the life of silence demanded by virginity of heart, to be guardians of this silence for one another. This silence, it should be added, neither excludes nor hinders the delicate attentions of self-forgetting love; on the contrary, it fosters them by making each person always ready to perceive the needs and desires of the other.

CHAPTER 5

Mary's Love
Becomes Sacrificial

We have seen something of that virginal love which was the tap-root of Mary's spirituality; now we must examine the development it underwent as Mary passed from childhood to adulthood. In particular, we must see how this love which had been predominantly passive took on a more active character — how virginal love inevitably became sacrificial love.

Mary's initial love was passive in two ways. First, there is the passivity essential to all supernatural love, inasmuch as the latter is a gift of God. It always has to be received in the actual moment, and the more it grows, the more it requires a passivity keeping us constantly subject to the action of the Holy Spirit.

Secondly, love was given to Mary initially, as we have seen, in the form of an infant's love for its mother. From the very outset, it infinitely transcended the natural gestures in which it was incarnate. These gestures were not, strictly speaking, signs expressive of love; a baby does not need signs, it cannot even recognize them. *Reason* needs signs, but a baby is satisfied with the natural evidence of love itself. And in Mary grace was always ahead of nature. The Holy Spirit's action preceded the infant Mary's first natural love for her mother, supernaturalizing it, and thereby sanctifying Mary's relations with her mother. Mary was an instrument of God for her mother far more than her mother was for her. The attitude of an infant is very meaningful for us, and we have already shown how Providence has arranged for this to be so.

Nevertheless, this attitude cannot be an adequate sign of supernatural love, because perfect love implies reciprocity. Hence when Mary reached adolescence, she realized that God had put capacities of love in her, not only in view of passivity and recollection, but also in view of an *effective* gift, i.e., for the active service of others, and above all for a complete gift of her own being. Love aroused in Mary the desire to serve. More and more, she realized that love is a union completed in actual giving.

In his infinite mercy for his created daughter, God not only wanted to love her and draw her to himself, he also asked her to give herself to him in an effective way by serving others. This action was not sought for itself or even for the results it produced, but as an expression of service and devotion, of self-denial and sacrifice. Mary was a handmaiden; she was one of those "unprofitable servants" (Luke 17:10) who allow God to use them for any service whatsoever, without laying any claim on him.

However, the goal of these new aspirations Mary experienced was much more profound and mysterious than simple service. Through that pure inner consciousness which was hers because of her virginal love, Mary discovered, in adolescence, the immense capacities of tenderness, compassion and generosity, that are to be found in a virginal body. She married Joseph in order that the mysterious capacities of love she was beginning to realize might be devoted exclusively to God through her vow of virginity. Daily she sensed more acutely how jealously God reserved to himself everything connected with that virginal spring within her which had belonged to him from the first instant of her life. The Holy Spirit made her acutely aware of the gratuitous character of this love which constantly brought her back to God in solitude and silence — the only condition in which she could be conscious of being totally given to her God, completely surrendered to him as a veritable slave of love.

At the same time, however, Mary sensed keenly that this interior union in the silence of prayer needed to be consummated in an effective gift which would express this love in her real life. But what sign could be adequate for a union so interior and so total? The good deeds done for her neighbor were altogether inadequate to satisfy the thirst for a gift of self, and for a total sacrifice, which the Holy Spirit aroused in her. They did not satisfy the need she experienced to express her love in her actual life.

In trying to determine as exactly as possible what the vow of virginity meant to her, we must distinguish between those matters about which the Holy Spirit gave her an express awareness and those about which she had no more than a presentiment. Her magnanimous love must at times have had presentiments of what was to come. At times these may even have turned into ardent desires, under the inspiration of the Spirit of God. But such desires were not so much acts of hers as of the Holy Spirit desiring in her; hence, even though extremely ardent, and at times full of light, these desires could plunge back again into the darkness of faith and the silence of love. Mary did not know exactly how God would fulfill them until the actual moment of realization.

We have already seen that, because of her love, she did not have the same sense of time and space that we do. She experienced a union in love in which there were also presentiments and desires springing from love. At any given moment, she was aware only of that which the Holy Spirit made explicit for her. The path by which the Spirit led his bride was not that of the prophets but that of the Queen of Prophets. It was not a pathway of light. This she did not need, because he dwelt within her and always led her in the actual moment with that embrace of love that characterizes the unitive life. Mary was able to remain a child forever in regard to everything in her personal life. Thus, her faith was so much the more meritorious, and the humility of the handmaiden lay precisely in renouncing any desire to clarify these presentiments on her own. Nevertheless, her intimate knowledge of Infinite Love made her sense that, even though the Holy Spirit was plunging her more and more deeply into the attitude of a child, he could also employ all the potentialities that she was beginning to discover in herself so as to give her new forms of love.

Here we will try to see what was in Mary's mind explicitly, and leave till later the question of presentiments about her virginal motherhood.

Love and Death

It was in adolescence, we may suppose, that Mary, through the wisdom of the Spirit, became aware of death. There is a 'death of love,' that is the peaceful, gentle death of our faculties of knowledge and action in Infinite Love. This she had known even as a child. But there is another death which is a punishment for sin: the violent separation of the soul from the body, with its consequence, the separation of the body from God's love when the body is in the tomb.[13] This must have been extremely mysterious for one who was sinless.

A child does not fear death. The little Christian in particular sees only the supernatural aspect of death, he does not realize its painful side. He knows of it merely as a blessed return to our Heavenly Father, where we will be close to Mary and the infant Jesus. True fear of death does not arise until reason has begun to operate, and one has developed a certain awareness of life and of that vital force in the body in which reason senses a kind of infinity. This seems to be why the sense of death develops at adolescence, along with an awareness of the powers of destruction both in and around us.

How did Mary become aware of death? How did the Holy Spirit give her, through her virginal love, an understanding of all that Scripture teaches about death as a consequence of sin? This is a mystery peculiar to the life of the Immaculate Virgin. Since she was Immaculate, it would appear that by rights she ought not to have died. Her body was already supernaturalized by the divine love that transfused and enveloped it. Of course, she was capable of physical suffering; but she did not experience the "death wish," or depressive tendencies, or the destructive impulse, with which some temperaments react to suffering and disappointment. Neither did she have that exultant *joie de vivre* which leads some people to revel in life for life's sake. In what way then, and by what means, did the Spirit of God make her aware, even before the coming of Jesus, of the forces of death and destruction at work in the world?

In the lives of the saints, we find extremely different attitudes toward death. Some of them seem to be spared, at least at certain periods of their life, from distinct consciousness of the painful aspect of death. God asks of them, and gives to them, the child's attitude of trust and self-surrender. They have an actual awareness only of the supernatural and consoling aspect of death as a meeting with God. They see it as a fuller degree of the 'death of love.' The terrifying aspects lie dormant in a love which prevents the reason and imagination from fixing their regard on them.

Sometimes, however, God maintains in his saints a keen awareness and painful fear of death as suffering and separation (which are what chiefly differentiate physical death from the 'death of love'). Sometimes divine love gives a veritable anguish at the thought of death, divesting us of all the illusions which the ego has instinctively built up around it to keep it out of our minds. This is particularly the case of the mystic, in whom the realism of love may turn the fear of death into a kind of agony, if God sees fit to let him experience its penal aspect. The love of God can give us a special realism about our own death and that of those near to us. Then it becomes a powerful means of purification; for the anguish seems to be bound up with the death of the ego and of that hope in life which makes us believe that death is not for us — at least not now. Finally, the Holy Spirit can make us experience in and through his love the suffering Jesus himself underwent at Gethsemani. This enables the friends of Jesus to offer it in union with him as the supreme matter of sacrifice.

As a magnanimous queen, Mary had to know the full depth and range of suffering undergone by her brothers and sisters. Her motherhood here on earth had to be crowned by the mystery of the Compassion. Surely the Holy Spirit must have made her aware of death, the matter of sacrifice *par excellence*, even during the preparatory phase of her life, i.e., prior to the Annunciation? Was it not in line with God's intentions for her that she become aware of it before receiving the grace of divine motherhood? This would have been the final preparation for her role.

Death would have appeared much more terrible in the mind and heart of Mary than it does for us. St. Thomas holds that the virtuous man fears death because he sees the body as an instrument for the acquisition of virtue and merit, whereas the barbarian exposes himself to death without fear.[14]

For a sinless being such as Mary, the body was intimately bound up with her life of love; it was substantially one with it. The deeply interior love-filled consciousness that God had given her, and in which he ceaselessly maintained her, divested her of all cogitation and images. She was immersed in an ardent, yet peaceful and recollected love which embraced her entire body. In the 'death of love' mentioned above, God asked of Mary the 'loss' of her soul; her body, however, was completely in the power of love and wholly unified by its union with God in love. Like the bride in the Song of Songs (5:2), it slept, but the heart kept vigil.

The violent separation of body and soul which occurs in physical death is quite different. Separated from the soul, the body is no longer under the dominion of the Holy Spirit, and so falls into decay. For Mary's virginal love, physical death could be the matter of sacrifice only by some exception. And yet, was it not the only sign, and the only determinate matter, which corresponded adequately to the thirst for an effective gift of self which she experienced?

Martyrdom

There is no greater proof of love than to give one's life for those one loves. Listening to the story of the Maccabees, for example, surely Mary must have had some presentiment of the mystery for which she was destined. She must have seen the mother of the Maccabees as an elder sister, not only lovable and admirable, but imitable. The violent death of martyrdom, which makes possible the greatest gift of self, is what corresponded best to the longing for humility and sacrifice that sprang from her virginal love.

We suppose that Mary's virginal body was intimately connected with the growth and expression of her love; at the same time we must recall that this body was capable of suffering. In fact, the love which permeated and enveloped her body made it all the more delicate and vulnerable. Mary welcomed this sensitivity to suffering because it provided her with a new possibility of giving herself. Furthermore, a sacrificed heart is more passive. A heart crushed by grief and bruised by suffering tends to be more sensitive to the movement of the Holy Spirit. Activity is always liable to harden us, because it entails a certain reaction, whereas suffering, when rightly endured, increases passivity, which is essential to love.

In divine love, even though it is essentially passive, Mary discovered a new kind of strength — one that can affect a person even physically. Its finest work appears in the martyrs, those heroes of the faith who display both strength and passivity as they confront their executioners. To Mary, the body offered two possibilities of martyrdom: a bloody martyrdom under the external assault of God's enemies, and a new 'death of love,' not in the sweetness and rest of recollection, but in the violence of a burning ardor so fierce the body cannot withstand it, so that the heart bursts.

On the cross, Jesus seems to have undergone this double martyrdom. The loud cry which he emitted before expiring was, according to St. Thomas, a sign of the vigor still left in his body.[15] Completely impregnated with love, his body withstood the external violence of the most terrible torments. It gave up life freely and voluntarily when its hour had come, under the inner violence of that infinite love it experienced when the Holy Spirit poured his love with unprecedented ardor into this passible body.

Jesus' cry was a cry of love. It was a sign that his death was not simply the martyrdom of an apostle, but a voluntary sacrifice, the loving sacrifice of the Bridegroom giving himself, his own body, to God for the sake of his bride. Mary alone understood the mysterious significance of this last call of Jesus as he confronted the immensity of evil. It was a call addressed to all men of good will, to his most intimate friends, and to the love and mercy of his Father.

When, at the dawn of adolescence, Mary began to experience the new vitality which love imparted to her body, she must have thirsted for this double martyrdom. In fact, this thirst can be regarded as the inspiration and goal of her vow of virginity, giving the vow its full meaning at each moment. The extent of her vow was to reserve for God alone all the capacities of her body, especially those new energies discovered through her virginal love, which the Holy Spirit used to show her the meaning of death in her desire for martyrdom.

This made the body appear to her still more mysterious. It was the bearer of potentialities, the extent of which she could not even glimpse. Yet she was certain that she ought to consecrate everything exclusively to the Spirit of God who had already taken possession of her entire being. She experienced a deep inner hope that he would respond to this offering and this interior sacrifice by giving her a new gift, the final beatitude of this life: that of the twofold martyrdom. Beyond that, it served to show her that God, who had already enriched her so much, had nothing more to give her.

Part Two

♣

The Annunciation: A New Revelation of God

CHAPTER 6

The Significance
of the Angel

Jesus was the divine response to this first attempt at religious life undertaken by Mary and Joseph. He was the fruit of a life which seemed sterile, which had been sacrificed voluntarily, and which looked solely to the Spirit of God for its fecundity. His coming did not withdraw Mary from her life of virginity, poverty, obedience and humility, but consecrated it, because he now shared it with her and enabled her to find new fruit-fulness in it.

Before the Annunciation, Mary's relationship with Joseph was like a preparation or step toward something unknown even to her. Without being able to see where she was going, she trusted in the Spirit of God who directed her by his interior promptings. The coming of Jesus, however, made it clear that Mary's religious life was the mysterious goal of the entire economy of revela-tion. The Father's plan, thwarted once through original sin, is here realized in a higher and better way.

Through the grace of the Immaculate Conception, the Holy Spirit already dwelt permanently in Mary. He led her to choose a way of life which would put her exterior ac-tivity and its framework into the fullest possible harmony with her interior condition. Mary's intention was to prepare a kind of little oasis in the midst of this world of sin — a place that would be in complete harmony with the inspirations of the Spirit, so that he could come to dwell there. The Holy Spirit responded to her resolve by a new gift to his bride. Even though she did not yet know him as a person distinct from Father and Son, she al-ready had faith in his mysterious calls; she had left everything to follow him. His response was to come and dwell in her in a new way, with a new fullness. Even before receiving explicit knowledge of the mystery of the Blessed Trinity, Mary had exercised faith in the 'invisible mission'[16] of the Holy Spirit. He responded to this heroic faith by making her the Mother of the Word through the visible mission of the latter.

But before bringing Mary's faith to fulfillment, the Annunciation was a trial for it. The Gospel tells us that she "was troubled" at the angel's greeting (Luke 1:29). It is important for us to see why this was so. Since Jesus did not live by faith, but had the beatific vision from the first moment of his earthly existence,[17] it is Mary who ranks first among believers. She is Queen of the faithful. This gives her faith a unique importance. The Annunciation, being the supreme trial of her faith — to say nothing of her entire life — was by the same token decisive for the destiny of all mankind, and of the entire universe.

In our efforts to understand all the dimensions of this trial, we need to separate its various aspects and examine them one by one. We will deal first with the difficulty that came from the presence of the angel, then with the problem inherent in his message, and finally with the anxiety resulting from Mary's relationship with Joseph. But in discussing these points thus distinguished from one another, we must bear in mind that in reality the Holy Spirit unified them by his love.

The presence of the angel Gabriel at the Annunciation seems to have been a factor in the trial of Mary's faith over and above the difficulty of the message itself. The fact that Mary was troubled at the angel's greeting suggests that, prior to the Annunciation, Divine Wisdom had led her without any miracles, apparitions or other extraordinary events. As first among the faithful, she had a mystical life greater than that of all the saints together; but for this very reason, she did not need any extraordinary manifestations such as interior words, visions or dreams. The Holy Spirit had directed her by communicating himself to her in a purely interior way. He developed her mystical spirit, as we have seen, by giving her a keen sense of silence and interiority, and drawing her ever more deeply into the intimacy of Divine Love. At the Annunciation, however, the angel appeared to her exteriorly. The sight of him, instead of giving her peace, troubled her. Perhaps she wondered whether he was a messenger of God or of the devil, for she would not have been unaware of the danger that evil spirits may disguise themselves as angels of light.

A much greater difficulty came from the apparent change in God's way of dealing with his beloved daughter. Up to now, the Spirit of God had spoken to the heart of his beloved and revealed his secrets to her without using any created intermediaries. Now, however, for the greatest secret of all, in comparison with which the others were mere preparations, Mary was obliged to trust a messenger who came between herself and her God. When someone shares a great secret with a dear friend, ordinarily he does this directly, not through an intermediary as God was doing here in the revelation of his most unfathomable secret.

The difficulty Mary experienced at this is very human. Many Christians feel the same difficulty in regard to the Church: it is hard to accept a teaching authority in matters of faith, and to recognize human beings as bearers of this authority.

In the wisdom of his love, and in order to develop Mary's faith, God did not address her directly, as a Father might out of consideration for the frailty of his little daughter. In this marriage proposal which he presented to her, he observed, as it were, an official protocol, one recognized by tradition. The act was not to remain hidden; and Mary's answer, which had public implications, had to be formulated in language that was external and definite. A hidden, interior response of the heart was not enough. (The angel does not seem to have appeared to her in a dream, or to have been merely imaginary, but to have come in a bodily form, as a real ambassador from God.) Also, in using an angel as intermediary between himself and mankind, God seems to have respected the order of nature. The angel, however, humbly recognized Mary as his Queen in the order of grace. "Hail, full of grace" he says. This was his name for Mary, the one that explained her queenship over him.

There is likewise a certain fittingness that an angel should have a role to play in a moment of Salvation History that was decisive for all creation. Also, the Incarnation of Jesus and, perhaps even more, the motherhood of Mary must have been a kind of scandal for the angels. This may have been the issue in the terrible warfare between the good and the fallen angels described by St. John in the Apocalypse (12:7ff.). Throughout the history of the world and of humanity, the good angels have been God's instruments in preparing the masterpiece planned by God in creation, while the wicked angels employ all the power they have left to act on the elements or on men so as to contravene or delay the accomplishment of God's plan. And just as the Incarnation of the Word through the motherhood of Mary had been the occasion of the angels' trial of faith, it was in turn an angel who constituted a trial for Mary's faith through his role of announcing to her these very works of the divine plan.

God sent Mary an angel, so that through this trial, she should become a queen to be venerated by angels as well as by men. Moreover, by her trust in God, the Queen of angels and men made a kind of compensation for the double infidelity of the angel and of Eve. She was the Morning Star, destined to take the place of Lucifer, who, according to tradition, had been the first of the angels, as the name of "light-bearer" suggests.[18]

The angel came to her while she was alone, and posed a problem of conscience which she had to resolve by herself. She was not allowed to consult anyone, not even Joseph, nor to continue in prayer to seek more light. The heavenly messenger asked for a definite answer at once. Mary realized that her reply would commit her whole life, interior as well as exterior, and would involve not only her relations with the Spirit of God but also those with others. It may also have seemed as though this new way of life would oblige her to give up the hidden life that had become so dear to her.

The King of Kings was treating his daughter like a queen. She was indeed a queen in the realm of love, and she was always led by the Holy Spirit in a truly royal fashion in the domain of her interior life. Until this moment, however, she had always been able to retain the attitude of a child and a disciple in the realm of faith and in her exterior life. All of her interior inspirations had been approved and confirmed by an exterior authority, and carried out with the support of this authority.

The Holy Spirit had already been using the revelations of the prophets to educate her; but in embracing them, Mary had had merely to rely like a child on the authority of a tradition received in faith. She did not have to pass judgment on the tradition. The Holy Spirit, shedding his interior light on this objective doctrine transmitted by her ancestors, had made Mary aware of the secrets hidden in the Word of God. He made her live them in the present moment and in the darkness of faith. She had not tried to articulate what she felt in her heart; on the contrary she had immersed herself in these blessed shadows, in which the poverty and nakedness of faith made her the least of all God's children.

If the Holy Spirit had already impelled Mary to adopt a radically new lifestyle, this was merely to enable her to surrender herself with complete liberty of soul to the silent intimacy of a contemplation which has no other aim but love. In her life with St. Joseph, there was a kind of division of functions. Joseph was God's representative for all that had to do with her exterior life. He was a kind of private prophet whom God had given as her lord and master. It was his responsibility to direct their household both in its communal life and in its relationships with society.

Thus the interior domain of Mary's soul had been in complete harmony with the exterior conditions of her life. The aspirations springing from her love, and her entire unitive life with God in the inner cell of her heart, were in full accord with the visible representatives of God on whom, as a child, Mary had been happy to rely.

But now she was obliged to conduct herself as Queen in the domain of faith also. In this supreme trial of her faith, she had to answer for herself. She had to show herself Queen of the faithful, Queen of believers. Her faith remained in the dark — in fact, it was darker than ever; yet she had to make a decision all by herself about an article of faith presented by God's messenger.

Before pursuing this line of thought any further, we must examine the contents of the angel's message, and the way Mary was prepared to receive it.

CHAPTER 7

Mary's Presentiments About Her Divine Motherhood

Mary was prepared for the divine motherhood by the unique grace of the Immaculate Conception. But we must ask whether the Holy Spirit did not prepare her in another way also, by the presentiments to which we have already alluded in considering how her virginal love developed from infancy onward.

In mystical graces, God sometimes begins by giving a faint light which, as we adhere to it, grows stronger. We can thus be led to discover new aspects of our faith that give it greater fullness. It remains essentially the same act of faith in the Word of God or in his inner witness; but its express contents are enriched or deepened by new perspectives given by love. They may be so clear as to be almost evident; or they may be no more than presentiments of something very remote.

The saints, especially those led by God in a privileged way from their earliest years, often seem to have had presentiments of their future calling. These presentiments may have been obscure, but could nevertheless be accompanied by intense desires. Exceptions to this general rule seem to have been due mainly either to infidelities or to the danger of pride and presumption, neither of which factors entered into Mary's case. The reason for this way of proceeding seems to be that God wants his saints to have the double merit of faith and hope — something made possible by the obscure presentiments given from the outset: "The end is present from the beginning." Divine Wisdom seems to dispose things in such a way that the end eternally predestined should be present in the intention, i.e., in the free and conscious desire, of the rational creature.

Though Mary was the humblest of creatures, her humility was magnanimous. Was not the virginal love which kept her centered on the "one thing necessary" by that very fact magnanimous? Mary's magnanimity came directly from her love. And was it not the magnanimity of her love that lay at the origin of her humility? This is another note peculiar to the spirituality of the Immaculate Virgin.

Furthermore, in Mary, the Holy Spirit acted in advance of nature. From the beginning of her life, even before she was able to reflect upon herself, he established her in that first love which she was never to lose. She is the one saint who never looked at herself; in her there was no turning back upon self. Her humility was above all an aspect of her mystical love. It was the passivity and loving docility which are like the mode which divine love takes in a creature that is led by God without any concern for self.

Mary had no desires of her own; her desires were the work of the Holy Spirit in her. The obscure presentiments and spontaneous desires of her soul did not arise from her ego (she had none), but from her love. This love was absolutely free to engender the most immense desires, with no concern for any human conditions extraneous to love itself: it took account of nothing but her fullness of grace. Mary did not limit or diminish God's calls by any reflection upon herself. Consequently, the only index by which we can gauge the range and depth of the Holy Spirit's desires in her is her fullness of grace.

Thus, for her, humility meant letting herself be led by God, with no resistance or initiative of her own. God knew that she was a poor creature; but he also knew the possibilities he had put into his creatures, particularly the human creature composed of body and soul. The human body possesses the infinite capacity of prime matter — a capacity beyond the grasp of any created intelligence, known to God alone. Would it not be an injustice to God, and to his infinite love, to wish on our own to limit the possibilities of his love in us? Mary's trust in this infinite love surpassed even her humility, and constantly enfolded it, because in all things she looked first to God. She knew her Beloved before anyone else; she did not even know herself except in him, in her love relationship with him.

Magnanimity was characteristic of her boundless trust, which comprised both total self-surrender and loving desire. In her the virtue of hope, in the form of confident trust, was marked by these two notes stirred up by the Holy Spirit. In short, the Holy Spirit had united her with God in such a way that everything in her was attracted by, and reached out toward, him. Her humility lay in maintaining the magnanimous attitude in which love had placed her.

Prepared by Love

It would seem normal that, as Queen of Love, Mary should have had some awareness of God's predilection for her, and of her unique place in the economy of salvation. Love seems to imply an awareness of having been chosen, and of the predilection of the one who has done the choosing. Mary's humility meant not looking at others on her own, not comparing herself with them; it made her stay in relationship solely with God and with those to whom God had joined her. But the magnanimity of her love postulated that she be aware of her love-relationship with God.

Mary's first love had been that of the little child who already loved God infinitely more than she loved even her mother. She loved him as if he were a mother, we may say; but in her virginal love the intensity of a spouse was added to the affection of an infant. Up until the Annunciation, her whole life had consisted in deepening and intensifying the essential characteristics of this virginal love, and had culminated in her vow of virginity.

If Mary's humility consisted in remaining docile under the ascendancy of the Holy Spirit, this means in effect that she never anticipated on her own initiative the presentiments and desires which came from him. Similarly, she did not try to specify or concretize them by her reason or imagination, e.g., by assimilating her case to that of the prophets. With still more reason, humility forbade her ever to restrain the impulses of the Holy Spirit out of human fear or faintheartedness. The Holy Spirit continually went beyond the desires of the Immaculate Virgin. He seemed to consider nothing but his immense love for her, as if paying no attention to her weakness.

Mary let him synthesize all the figures and predictions of the prophets in and through the virginal love he had inspired in her. She was not master of the love within her, but its humble servant. She had offered to God her whole being, and her body in particular, as a little earth on which he could come to dwell. She allowed Divine Love to enter into her — almost to turn into her — and take hold of all the capacities of a matter which had been created especially for this divine service of love. And Divine Love, after entering into Mary and transforming the matter provided by her, carried her off with itself.

In this circle of love, Mary's part was merely that of the "unprofitable servant" (Luke 17:10). Nevertheless, she gave her *fiat* freely, as one lovingly conscious of the love of her God. She was also a magnanimous servant, who gave thanks for the power and condescension of that Infinite Love which could fashion the most beautiful masterpiece out of next to nothing. Thus by her virginal love Mary was prepared for the great revelation which was to take place at the Annunciation. The development of love throughout her life had brought her closer and closer to it. The Holy Spirit completed this preparation by the new ardor which she experienced under his inspiration and the presentiments to which it gave rise.

Queen of the Prophets

Mary's Jewish faith and hope naturally oriented her toward the Messiah. By the mouth of the prophets, the Holy Spirit had announced him as closer and closer. But it was chiefly through the inner, invisible mission of the Holy Spirit that Mary had grown more and more aware of his imminent coming. Her virginal love was waiting, yearning, calling for him. She thirsted for him — the only one who could satisfy the ardor of her longing that grew daily more intense.

The prophets had received from the Spirit the mission of preparing for the coming of the Messiah by their words. Mary had the mission of hastening his coming by her contemplative silence. In the designs of Providence, there was an interval between the prophets and the Messiah; this was Mary's moment. Must she not have had some consciousness of this mission throughout her life?

According to St. Thomas, the full charism of prophecy is differentiated from a mere prophetic impulse by the consciousness and certitude which the prophet has of God's intervention.[19] Surely the Queen of Prophets had this prophetic consciousness more than anyone else! However, it was by her silence — the silence of love, of her virginal love — that Mary was Queen of Prophets, the one in whom the Spirit dwelt in all his fullness. And this virginal love was linked with her Immaculate Conception. This suggests that the Father wanted her to prepare for the coming of his Son from the beginning of her life as Queen of Love, conscious of her mission. But even though the love which suffused Mary's entire life made her much more certain of the presence of the Spirit of God in her than the prophets had ever been, it did not give her an explicit knowledge of specific matters of faith except insofar as God was pleased to bestow this. Her awareness was the sort proper to the unitive life.

Thus, her consciousness of her mission, although quite certain, was at first only implicit. Gradually, however, it became more and more explicit as she listened to the Scriptures and as her virginal love deepened with advancing age.

Preparing for His Coming

The proper mystery of that first period in the life of the immaculate Queen of the Prophets would seem to have consisted in this, that while she always lived wholly in the present moment, the Holy Spirit caused her also to relive the entire purgative and illuminative phases of the history of Israel, as experienced by the prophets and people. This continued until the moment when her love became so strong and violent that it could no longer remain here on earth without being actually united to the Divine Word, Subsistent Truth himself. The invisible mission of the Holy Spirit had become so profound and intense that it could no longer stay hidden under the figure and symbols of the prophets. The Word himself had to come and replace these figures and symbols through his

77

visible mission. Mary's intense desire hastened his coming. He was to be *her* savior before all others. If he had waited any longer, her languishing love itself would have made a martyr of her. The impetuous desires incited by the Holy Spirit would have brought her to death by a martyrdom of love.

But what concretely was her relationship with him to be? Was it her role simply to prepare for his coming in a purely contemplative way, in the passivity of love, letting the Holy Spirit hasten the time through her prayerful desires? Or was he asking something more of her? Would her love be called upon to assume a more active mode?

Mother of the Messiah?

We cannot exclude the possibility that Mary received some presentiment that she was to be the Mother of the Messiah. If Simeon had been given the assurance that he would not taste death before seeing the Christ (Luke 2:26), is it not likely that Mary would have received a similar foreboding? To her conscious mind, it may well have seemed in contradiction with her call to virginity; but indications from the Lord often seem contradictory to reason or common sense.

How such a thing could come about, she would have had no idea; but she may have sensed that it would involve an immense sacrifice. Other Israelite maidens dreamed of bearing the Messiah, King of Glory. Mary had a truer sense of the fate that awaited him. From the prophet Isaiah she knew of the "Servant of Yahweh" who was to be repudiated by the very people to whom he brought salvation by bearing their guilt (Isaiah 52:13-53:12). Israel at large had not identified this mysterious figure with the Messiah; but this does not mean that Mary missed the link between them. Jesus called his disciples "foolish and slow of heart to believe all the prophets have said" (Luke 24:25) when they failed to recognize that "it was necessary that the Christ should suffer." Mary's heart, which had not been dulled by sin, may not have been so slow to perceive the true sense of those Scriptures which, addressed to the whole people of Israel, were meant above all for her. The promised Messiah had already been given to her heart. He was far more precious to her than her own life. Without understanding how or why, she already loved him with the heart of a mother and a bride, and generously embraced his sufferings.

We have already seen how, as an adolescent, Mary felt a growing desire to fulfill her intimate union of love with God (and thus with the Messiah who, in her love, was one with God) by an effective gift, a gift of her own life in sacrifice or martyrdom. Perhaps she sensed obscurely that she was called to realize this, not directly in her own flesh, but by furnishing the sacrificial victim. By associating the Suffering Servant of Isaiah with the Song of Songs and with the mother of the Maccabees, the Holy Spirit could have given her such a presentiment, along with the yearnings which were more and more ardent as the coming of the Messiah drew near. And when in fact the Spirit made Mary a martyr through the Son of her virginal love, may he not have been responding to the ardent appeals of her magnanimous heart?

In any case, the Messiah was truly the child of Mary's heart before being born of her flesh. Her responsibility was to prepare her heart for his coming, by loving him already as a mother and as a bride. This was her one and only mission at that time. The Holy Spirit did not send her forth to proclaim his word; he asked her to receive him, and the teaching he had given through the prophets, as a humble servant, a mere disciple, but also as a mother and bride. And the infant love which he had given her at the beginning of her life contained this double virtuality: the humility of the servant and the magnanimity of the bride. These two qualities were combined in a single attitude, simpler and more divine than either of them alone — the attitude which arose naturally and spontaneously from her virginal love.

CHAPTER 8

The Divine Motherhood: Realization of Mary's Presentiments

"Do not be afraid, Mary, you have found favor with God. You will be with child and give birth to a son, and you are to give him the name Jesus. He will be great and will be called the Son of the Most High. The Lord God will give him the throne of his father David, and he will reign over the house of Jacob forever; his kingdom will never end."

* * *

"The Holy Spirit will come upon you, and the power of the Most High will overshadow you. So the holy one to be born will be called the Son of God."
— Luke 1:30-35

It is difficult to determine what Mary would have understood from these words of the angel. That she was to conceive a child by the action of the Holy Spirit is clear; that he would be the Messiah was unmistakable for a mind steeped in the traditions about the promised Son of David. But in what sense would she have understood his being "Son of God"? Neither exegetes nor theologians are in agreement on this question.

Objectively considered, the angel's statement embraces the two major Christian doctrines of the Trinity and the Incarnation. It does not do so in the person/nature language of later theology, of course, but that is beside the point. The substance of these mysteries is there, in what is said about the Son of God being born of Mary through the working of the Holy Spirit. The terms Trinity and Incarnation, as well as all the definitions about person, processions, nature, etc., are merely instruments invented by theologians to enable them to grasp and — according to the methods of their discipline — to grapple with the great realities of faith which were originally revealed in the simple concrete terms of human experience.

Likewise, when we ask whether Mary, in listening to the angel's words, perceived these profound truths, we do not envisage her being able to conceptualize them in the language of the fourth-century Greek theologians. We must suppose that she assimilated the revelation in the very terms in which it was announced to her. The problem is that the laconic message of the angel is susceptible, of itself, of being understood at two levels. It could be understood in a relatively superficial sense to mean simply that the conception of the child would be brought about by a miraculous operation of the divine power. Or it could be understood in the profound sense that the child to be born of her would be the Son of God in the fullest, most proper sense of the word, namely, that to God the Father there is born one who is of the very same nature as himself, while being really distinct from him. Even to express this distinction, we are obliged to have recourse to a language in which Mary, of course, would not have articulated it. More succinctly, the question is, did Mary realize that her son would be divine, or merely that he would be produced by God without the cooperation of a human father? In past ages, preachers and theologians tended to assume the former; today they tend to be far more skeptical about it.

Since, at the finding of the child Jesus in the Temple, Luke tells us that Mary and Joseph "did not understand what he was saying to them, but that Mary "treasured all these things in her heart" (Luke 2:50, 51; cf. 2:19), it is plausible that the same was true in the present instance, but that still does not tell us precisely what Mary understood. In any case, let us beware of the common trap of arguing from what would have been understood by the ordinary Hebrew maiden of her time. Whatever else she was, Mary was not an ordinary Hebrew, above all when it came to receiving the Word of God; rather, it is precisely in this that she was the most "blessed among women" (Luke 1:42, cf. 45).

Hence we must suppose that Mary's reception of the Word of God was far more perceptive than that of anyone else. If the Trinity and the Incarnation were implicit in Gabriel's message, we cannot rule out a priori Mary's recognition of them. And when you consider the actual ways of God in Salvation History, it seems utterly inadmissible that Mary should have been given the role of Mother of God, and brought into the incredibly human and intimate relationship with the Second Divine Person which this role entails, without being made aware of it. The very dynamics of the exchange between Gabriel and Mary indicate that she was being called upon to give her consent freely and consciously.[20] But what would have been the meaning of such consent, if Mary did not know the most important and essential point about that to which it was given? She was told that the message was from God, and that God was pleased with her; can we suppose that it was kept hidden from her that God himself would be the term of the motherhood she was asked to accept? Especially when his identity is in fact given in the term "Son of God"? The God who addressed her through the words of Gabriel was not only her sovereign Lord, he was also the Beloved of her heart, to whom she was already espoused by her vow of virginity. Would he not have let her understand that this new and transcendent relationship to which he was now calling her was a relationship with himself?[21a]

On the grounds of such considerations, we will assume that Mary realized, in some real and decisive way, that the Son of God, who was now about to become her son, was in truth divine — the Son of God in a unique and proper sense. The simplest peasant knows what it means to be the son of someone, even if he cannot analyze it. Likewise he knows the difference between being son in a real sense, and son figuratively speaking. For Mary the message that God had a son, and that God's Son was to become her son also, was undoubtedly full of mystery; but we suppose that she grasped its truth. More truly than Peter, when he declared, "You are the Christ, the Son of the Living God" (Matthew 16:16); more profoundly than Thomas, when he exclaimed, "My Lord and my God" (John 20:28); Mary perceived that "the holy one to be born" would be in truth "the Son of God."

Farther on we will suggest how this may have come about. But assuming for now that this was the case, we *must regard the Annunciation as an epoch-making step in the history of Divine Revelation. Mary was the first person to whom God divulged these two inscrutable secrets of the divine life. Belief in them is what gave her faith its characteristic note and its special merit.*

But just as we said above that she would not have formulated these insights in the language of Nicaea, so we must add that she would not have viewed them in the perspective of an historian of doctrine. In fact, it seems inappropriate to speak of a perspective for her. This term evokes the image of a scholar, looking at revelation somewhat from the outside, either in function of its place in the system of truth, or by situating it in historical context. But the light in which Mary pondered all that God revealed to her was simply her virginal love. She contemplated revelation from within, from a divine point of view, which even the prophets did not have.[21b]

Mary's Preparation for the New Revelation

Of course, the Holy Spirit acts as an inner teacher for the prophets. He enlightens them interiorly, and confirms this light by his intimate presence, given through love. Nevertheless, it is merely for the sake of some function related to his people that he enlightens them. To Mary, he gave himself as a spouse, in his fullness. All the formation that she had received was a preparation for this fullness. She was the beloved daughter of the Father, called to be the mother and mystical bride of his Son.

Her virginal love had prepared her to receive the revelation of these two great mysteries. All the developments undergone by her love as she advanced in age made her more and more ready. The new ardor which she experienced in adolescence, along with all the presentiments engendered under the Spirit's inspiration, completed this divine preparation.

In any case, as she heard the words of the angel, Mary listened, above all with her heart, to their inner echo in her soul, where the Holy Spirit enjoyed an uncontested sovereignty. The message presented by the angel was a mixture of light and darkness. The presentiments we have suggested were at best very obscure. They remained hidden in the darkness of faith, as her humility kept her always in the present moment.

But when God's messenger called upon her to make the decision that was to determine the course of her entire life, these presentiments must have crystallized under the impulse of her love. Even if Mary had some previous intimation that she was to be Mother of the Messiah, she would not thereby have known that he was to be the Son of God. This is something she had to learn from the angel's statement, "The holy one to be born will be called the Son of God" (Luke 1:35). But in view of all that had prepared her mind and still more her heart for this moment, would not this new revelation have come as a kind of key that clarified all that had gone before it? Would it not have appeared as the only truth that corresponded to all the other factors, and gave them a satisfactory, objective meaning?

She may also have sensed that this was the marvelous solution of Divine Wisdom for giving her the merit of sacrifice, while keeping her in the humble role of a woman of those times, hidden in the home, apart from the combats and persecutions of the world. Likewise, it would reconcile the passivity essential to love with the longing for an effective and total gift of self which love engendered.

A New Intervention of the Spirit

Furthermore, we must suppose that, in addition to the exterior message of the angel, there occurred a new intervention of the Holy Spirit in Mary's soul. The exterior word and the interior inspiration complemented one another. Neither alone would have sufficed for the faith and the *fiat* asked of her. Without an interior experience of love, the angel's message would have been too implicit for Mary to be able to recognize expressly and certainly the revelation of the two great mysteries of the Blessed Trinity and the Incarnation. Modern exegesis has made this plain. Moreover, the angel did not proffer any visible miracle to prove that he was indeed God's envoy, and to give Mary's external senses some visible and tangible evidence. Hence it was necessary for the Holy Spirit himself to reassure his beloved interiorly by a new gift of his love.

But this new intervention of the Spirit was itself so mysterious that it demanded blind faith in Infinite Love. His action occurred in the darkness of a faith that was not yet fully explicit. Mary may well have been aware, in and by her love, of the miraculous conception which the Holy Spirit was bringing about in her. She may have realized that he was no longer content with a simple union of love (even one which embraced her entire being and filled her with ineffable peace), but now was revealing himself to her in a new, real and physical way. Her mystical spouse was giving her a child as the sign of their love, and to teach her a new degree of *littleness*, as will be explained shortly. But even if Mary was certain that this child of her love (the only one who was fully and purely a child of love in a world invaded by selfishness) was indeed the fruit of the Spirit, only the angel's message could disclose to her that he would be in fullest truth the Son of God, a person distinct from the Father and the Spirit. And even though this word came as the key to all the presentiments by which the Holy Spirit had been preparing her up to this point, still Mary had to make a special act of faith (and of hope) in what the angel now said to her expressly.

The Sign of the Infant Jesus

The revelation brought by the angel entailed a new purification of Mary's faith and hope. Her faith no longer had any human representation or intellectual consideration to support it. Mary had to rely solely on the love that dwelt within her, and which gave her God as her son. From now on she would have to rely on this infant that she did not yet see, whom she did not yet know, either by her senses, or by her imagination, or her reason, but only by her love.

This infant took even her littleness away from her. Ho longer was she the 'least' among the children of men. No longer had she the first place among little ones. She realized that hereafter she would have to take second place to her own child in this very intimate and royal domain in which previously she had had the glad sense of being the first. This brought both joy and reassurance to her magnanimous humility. The one created reality to which she could have become attached, had she ever contemplated herself, had now been taken away from her.

At the decisive moment of the Annunciation, the Holy Spirit must have given Mary a powerful inner awareness that her virginal motherhood would mean for her love the grace above all of a new birth and a new littleness. This is what impelled his spouse to pronounce gladly her definitive *fiat*. This motherhood would lead Mary still more deeply into the inner domain of poverty of spirit and humility of heart — the only one that counted for her. It would allow her to give place to one who was littler than she was, her little one who was infinitely little, with a divine littleness, and who attracted her so powerfully. From now on she would have to be his disciple and let herself be inspired, formed, shaped by him. Was this new littleness not the inner sign given Mary by the Holy Spirit, that it was indeed he who was acting within her? It harmonized with all that the prophets had said and with all the presentiments which the Holy Spirit had given her up to this point.

Let us try to see now how the Holy Spirit shed light on the angel's words, bringing Mary, through this mystery of littleness, to understand the two great mysteries of the Blessed Trinity and the Incarnation.

Jesus, Love as Fire

Mary had first come to know love in the form of the intimate relationship between the infant and its nursing mother. We have already seen, however, the inadequacy of this sign as an expression of Mary's love for God. There was a kind of disproportion between the interiority of this love, and the exteriority of the infant's relations with its mother. The infant is no longer in its mother's womb; although near her and carried by her, it is nevertheless exterior to her. But Mary's love for God was *interior*, with a divine interiority. Its opposite is not what we ordinarily call 'exterior', that is, exterior to knowledge and imagination. For the divine interiority of love, what is exterior is solely that which is alienated from love by the human will and ego.

At the Annunciation, a new love burgeoned within the first one. In and through love the Holy Spirit brought about the virginal conception of Jesus. The Spirit gave himself to Mary in a new form of love. Using the passivity characteristic of love, he actualized the mysterious capacities of Mary's being. Her love became productive and fruitful; it was no longer merely passive. Jesus was the blessed fruit of her womb. Jesus arose in her like a wound left by the fire of love — of another love which was interior like her own, but infinitely more intense. It was this love which revealed to her the presence of a new person, a divine person.

Theology has traditionally held that the soul of Jesus was created at the instant of the virginal conception of his body and, being united to the Divine Word from the moment of its creation, had the beatific vision from the outset of its existence.[22] From the beatific vision its fullness of grace and charity derived.[23] The same theology holds that Jesus must have been conscious of this fullness of grace in the very moment that he was sanctified by it.[24] How are we to understand this consciousness?

It had to be a mystical consciousness deriving from love and developing in love. Where knowledge is concerned, a distinction has to be made between Jesus' beatific vision and the other kinds of knowledge that he had as an earthly pilgrim. There is no corresponding distinction in the case of love. There was only one love which sprang directly from the beatific vision and from the depths of Jesus' soul, filling and enveloping his entire body by a touch that was wholly interior. It is this love that gave Jesus the consciousness or awareness that lay at the basis of his life as an earthly pilgrim. Love was the link between the beatific vision and all the perfections of Jesus the wayfarer. Love held the primacy over every form of knowledge in him. Thus it was mystical knowledge and the kind of awareness that arises from it that governed the entire life and growth of Jesus.

Jesus' first love was infinitely more perfect than Mary's. It would seem to have had a mode of its own that distinguished it from hers. Mary's first love was essentially passive, because she was in the regime of faith. Jesus, on the contrary, had the beatific vision. The form of love which flows from the beatific vision is not, properly speaking, passive. The passivity characteristic of the gifts of the Holy Spirit under the regime of faith does not obtain in the beatific vision. There, love is a fire.

In the body of Jesus, Divine Love seems to have found a matter that allowed it to turn into fire, a fire that was indeed mystical, yet nonetheless real. Since the body that was united hypostatically to the Word was a substantial part of Jesus' humanity, it was not merely *subjected* to a fire that remained really distinct from it and in contact with it; Jesus' body was taken into that fire, and became itself a substantial fire. In itself, the Divine Word is Substantial Light ("light from light" as we say in the Creed). In becoming incarnate in the body of Jesus, it became likewise a substantial fire, because this divine body was wholly penetrated by this fire. The Word could not yet give himself to Mary in the form of light, but through his body the light could be given to her in the form of fire. Or, the body of Jesus may be called a brazier, because it brought the fuel that allowed a fire to be lighted, so that Infinite Love could give itself under the sign of fire. But it is more than a sign, it is also a reality; this substantial fire burns whatever it touches.

Jesus, who came to set fire on the earth (Luke 12:49), could not wait to enkindle his mother, who was thirsting for this very fire. He came to quench the thirst of Mary's virginal soul and to satisfy those ardent new yearnings which nothing else here below could satisfy. This New Fire gave Mary the desire for martyrdom and for heaven. But heaven had come down to her; it was in truth the fire of heaven that enveloped and hid the Word himself. There was more fire at this Pentecost than at the later one, even though (or rather because) the fire was hidden — hidden in Mary's heart.

This burning love which surpassed, and by the same token appeased, the ardor of the adolescent Mary was the love of a tiny infant, one infinitely tinier than Mary herself had been at her birth. It was not an infant carried in her arms and united with her externally, but an infant she bore within her own body, and who, even more, bore her in his love. This love brought her new life, intensifying that love of hers which had been languishing for want of something to quench its thirst or appease its ardor. Jesus' very littleness was itself a sign for Mary. This inner sign which she felt in her own flesh — was it not the hidden sign that clarified the angel's words? In the light of love, her little one was a sign — a perfect sign because much more than a sign — the very reality of his own love, becoming life in her.

The Light Given to Mary

An unborn infant is one with the mother who carries it. Although two, they have only one life. By this experience the Holy Spirit led Mary into an understanding of the mystery of the Blessed Trinity and of the loving relationships by which the Divine Persons are interior to one another.

In the divine experience of the Annunciation, the Holy Spirit revealed himself to Mary in a new way, in the role of a spouse. Likewise, the infant Jesus made her aware, in and through her love, and by its very ardor, that he too was a divine person distinct from the Holy Spirit. Jesus revealed himself to Mary as wholly suffused with the love of the Spirit who conceived him. This same love united him to Mary. By it the Spirit of Jesus must have made her understand that love for the Father which keeps the Son and Spirit eternally present in the Father's bosom, just as they were pleased to make themselves consciously present in Mary's bosom now in time.

We pointed out above that Jesus' love, being a kind of fire, had a different mode from that passive love which Mary had received from the Holy Spirit. Should we not suppose that Mary's little one thereby made her understand that he was the *Verbum spirans amorem* — the "Word that breathes forth love"? He and the Father give the Holy Spirit to one another in a love called *active* (to distinguish it from love received as a gift).

Through the angel's words, together with the interior light of this divine experience, Mary came to realize that in God, love is not merely what theologians call the "subsistent universal good," or the "separated common good of the universe," toward which deficient and imperfect creatures are drawn. It is the intimate, interior bond between two persons joined in one living and luminous union as Father and Son. The Father engenders his Son, not out of the necessity of a nature needing to propagate itself or break out of its limits, not out of the need of knowledge to express itself, but out of a superabundance of life and light.

This Son, a luminous and living Word, remains eternally in the bosom of his Father. But in God, light and life are identical with love. The engendering of the Son is inspired by love and culminates in a gift of love that constitutes a new person: the Holy Spirit, the Divine Gift. It is not proper to speak of a 'common life' in God, because there is simply the one, single life of all three persons; nevertheless, *our* common life helps us draw near to God and prepares us for this unity of love. A life that is separate and egotistic, on the other hand, closes a person to the mystery of love.

In God there is a Word, but one that does not break the silence. It does not imply any division or exteriority, because it is an interior, substantial Word. It is likewise, as we have said, *Verbum spirans amorem,* a word that breathes love. It is inspired by love and uttered for the sake of a gift of love. This personal gift was given to Mary by the Father and the Son. The latter gave himself to her in an invisible mission from the first instant of his life in her. In and by the Holy Spirit, on the day of the Annunciation, Mary knew within herself the mystery of the Son eternally engendered by the Father. She did not know this in a clear light but in the poverty and humility of love — a love that had bent down to become incarnate in her womb.

This Son was the offspring of her flesh and of her love, the fruit of her faith and hope. In coming to know that the mystery of Infinite Love is beyond all created light and life, and that nothing but love can bring us an interior touch of God and mystical knowledge of him, Mary discovered that there is in God a substantial light and a substantial life identified with love. But she learned this in the darkness and poverty of faith, in the humility and patience of hope. Only in heaven does God give himself in light, in a life of light and glory. Here below, union with God in love demands the privation of every created light, and the sacrifice even of one's own life. Here on earth, eternal life begins in love, not in light.

Thus Mary perceived, with the clarity peculiar to love, that faith attains its perfection only in the nakedness of the present moment, and in a soul that consents to lose itself so that the spirit can adhere to God at its summit (or better, in its profoundest depths) by a touch of love that is substantial and interior. This touch involves no mental word or imaginary representation. It springs from love and subsists in a love that finds in the depths of our being a prime matter completely open to being pervaded by love. At this moment Mary understood why hope finds its ultimate perfection here below in an attitude that may be called 'divine patience.' This is the total passivity of a completely virginal love that surrenders itself entirely to the Divine Spouse, giving up all initiative of its own, stripped of every desire and every human joy, eager to be sacrificed by love.

Besides bringing her virginal love to fulfillment, the Annunciation revealed to Mary the meaning of the spiritual poverty and interior humility of her life of love which was likewise, in the economy of revelation, a life of faith and hope. The entire spirituality of the Immaculate Virgin can be perceived in the mystery of the Annunciation. The disclosure of the end which had secretly inspired and directed her spiritual life revealed the spiritual and mystical significance of this life — both its dogmatic foundation and the reason for the faith and hope which modified it. Thus the revelation made at the Annunciation was indeed the culmination of all that had gone before it. It was a culmination, however, not in glory and light, but in the fire of love. For this reason, it plunged Mary's faith and hope all the more deeply into poverty and humility.

The infant hidden in Mary's womb was also a sign shedding new light on the message of the prophets and on the whole of creation. Mary's virginal love had long since fixed deep in her heart the words of the prophet Isaiah (7:14): "The Lord himself will give you a sign: the virgin will be with child and will give birth to a son." These words were now illuminated for her; their meaning suddenly became clear. The key had been given to her in this sign which came like a blazing fire in the absolute midnight of faith. Her presentiments about the mystery of the adorable Trinity, which had been inspired by the whole inner life of her soul, were now fulfilled in a measure beyond anything she could have desired. It became perfectly clear to Mary that her interior experience of the Holy Spirit could not be explained adequately in terms of the notion of God presented by Hebrew tradition. The God made known to her by the Holy Spirit was an immanent God.

At the same time all her presentiments about the Messiah and his relations with his lowly servant were realized. The child in her womb was in fact the mystical spouse foretold by Hosea and the Song of Songs. He was the spouse of her virginal heart. In his overflowing love for his little child, this Divine Spouse had made himself even smaller than she in order to be able to come and dwell in her.

This Jesus, who was for her at one and the same time the least of the children of men and the most ardent of lovers, made her understand the connection between love and littleness. This tiny infant was indeed the Servant of Yahweh described by Isaiah, and the fire of his love already gave Mary a premonition of the mystery of his passion. The world that had not understood the prophets would not be able to receive his word of fire. At the same time, so burning a love could find nowhere but in martyrdom a visible sign capable of revealing the infinity of its love, especially to a world of sinners.

CHAPTER 9

The Crux of
the Annunciation

What was it in the Annunciation that presented the greatest difficulty to Mary's faith? At first glance, one might suppose it was the promise that she was to become a mother while remaining a virgin. But we must beware of trying to understand Mary's reactions in terms of ordinary human psychology, which is that of minds darkened and confused by sin. Mary was immaculate; the mentality in which she received the angel's message was that of the mystical life conferred by her privileged grace. Moreover, her mental attitudes had been formed by the biblical accounts of God's mighty works in favor of his people, such as the stories of the offspring given to the aged Sarah and to sterile Anna. She had been nurtured on the prophets, and the Holy Spirit had given her a kind of 'inside understanding' of them, synthesizing and illumining them in her mystical consciousness. She could not have been unaware of the mysterious passage of Isaiah 7:14, which we discussed above. More than any other passage of the Scriptures, it was meant for her. Hence the miracle of a conception wrought by the Holy Spirit would not have presented a major difficulty for her faith.

What was absolutely new for Mary was the fact that she was to be the Mother of God, and that her intimate love-relationships with her God were the prolongation in time of the eternal relations constituting the three Divine Persons. But even here, Mary's virginal love had purified her of our usual perspectives of quantity, exteriority and division. They had given her instead a keen sense for a new dimension of interiority and depth, of which the mystery of the Holy Trinity revealed to her the ultimate significance.

Furthermore, she already had a presentiment of the mysterious bonds between Infinite Love and the infinitely little, the infinity of God and the infinity of matter. Finally, and most important of all, the unique rule of life for this humble and magnanimous handmaid of the Lord was his will, his 'good pleasure,' as it was manifested to her in each actual moment. Thus her virginal love for the Father had prepared her fully to receive the gift of his Spirit with thanksgiving, and to become the beloved mother of his Son.

The two difficulties just mentioned were both intrinsic to the angel's message. Other difficulties lay, not in the message itself, but in the conditions under which it was presented. One consisted in the fact that it was presented by an angel; we have already touched on this. Another came from Mary's relationship with St. Joseph. This we must now examine at length, for this seems to be what constituted the supreme trial of Mary's faith at the Annunciation.

As was pointed out above, Joseph was head of the household: he held the authority over this common life which the two of them led under the inspiration of the Holy Spirit. Mary was subject to him; in the culture of that day, her situation was comparable to that of a child. Should the angel then not have addressed his request to Joseph first of all? At least, should he not have dealt with the two of them together about a request involving them both? Joseph was not merely the external head of this household of the hidden life; he was also the one that Mary, under the inspiration of the Holy Spirit, had chosen as the guardian of her virginity.

This explains some of Mary's perplexity with regard to the angel. If he were really a messenger from God, would he not (especially in an act that had, so to speak, an official character) respect the authority established by God? Should he not at least have made some mention of Joseph? His intervention appeared to violate the order of marriage inspired by the Spirit of God himself. If it does nothing else, Mary's trial should help us understand how God can lead us along paths which seem to be contradictory and to go against all human reason and logic.

This was a moment of veritable agony for Mary. The Holy Spirit, who always supported and consoled her interiorly, now seemed to leave her in perplexity and anguish, without giving any inner witness or indication of his will for her. For one who lived constantly in the presence of the Holy Spirit as she did, drawing her peace from it, finding in it the key to the attitude she should adopt in each situation, and in fact to her entire life, the veil which seemed to descend on this presence when the angel appeared must have doubled her perplexity and anguish. If this spirit was from God, why should his appearance diminish her sense of the presence of God? Joseph's presence always deepened her sense of peace and inner light; why was the presence of the angel so different? This was Mary's great trial.

God seems to have wanted Mary to make a decision on her own at this moment. She had to use her mind and will in an act of faith of which love was not the unique and sufficient inspiration. This must have been the only occasion, or one of the very few occasions, in Mary's life when the Holy Spirit did not intervene as her spouse, or at least as her counselor.

Such an interior trial seems presupposed by St. Luke's statement that Mary was "deeply troubled" at what the angel said to her (Luke 1:29). Mary's trouble suggests that God was treating her at this moment, not as queen in the realm of love, but as first in the line of believers, as mother of the faithful. He wanted her to know by her own experience the anguish so often undergone by her children — for example, by someone called by God to leave a religion which has served him for a while in a preparatory way. Even more particularly the mystics, who are particularly the children of Mary, undergo such anguish.

Likewise, Mary was experiencing in her own person the mystery of the passage from the Old Law to the New. As Mother and Queen of believers (even though in a hidden way), Mary had to live mystically all that this transition involved as intended by God. The Old Testament regime was essentially that of the purgative and illuminative life. The New Testament, in its deepest mystery, in the grace signified by its sacraments and proclaimed by the word of Jesus, is fully realized only in the unitive life, i.e., in a union with God that is wholly interior and hidden. From the outset of her life, Mary had been situated in the unitive way; but at the Annunciation she underwent a trial of faith similar to that experienced by the mystics when their ego is put to death as they pass from the purgative and illuminative ways to the unitive.

We may also say that the Annunciation amounted to a new birth — Mary's definitive birth in the realm of love. But prior to this birth, God let her experience the suffering and anguish of death.

What exactly was the source of Mary's anguish?

She was, of course, aware of the law of Moses, according to which a woman taken in adultery was to be stoned; she realized that her *fiat* could bring the death penalty upon her. But this is not what made her hesitate. If she had been certain about God's will in this matter, she would gladly have risked her life for him and been martyred for faith in him. Likewise, it is conceivable that God was allowing her to experience her own weakness and to be afraid; however, simple fear is not the same thing as anguish. The latter we experience only when life itself is threatened and we see no way to escape. In Mary's case, it was her life of faith that seemed threatened by an apparent violation of the regime which God himself had fixed for her, in giving Joseph authority over her external life.

Mary sensed that she had to reply immediately. She raised an objection, pointing out to the angel that she was a virgin, as a way of discerning from his reply whether he was truly the messenger of God. Mary was indeed the 'prudent virgin.' But did the angel's answer give her full light on this? Pupil of the Holy Spirit that she was, Mary would not have full assurance except through an inner witness, especially since there had been no miracle to give her a confirmation, and since she was aware of Satan's cleverness and the power left to him by God.

The Holy Spirit seems to have let Mary decide for herself, giving her some interior indication no doubt, but not enough to be decisive. Mary gave her *fiat* because, if a risk had to be taken, she preferred to expose herself to external hardship and embarrassment, should she be mistaken, rather than refuse a gift of God — especially one which, at this moment, appeared above all as a sacrifice. She was well aware that her life of grace was in no danger because of her complete good will in the matter. For nothing whatsoever would she give offense to God. If she were mistaken, if she involuntarily became the devil's plaything, she alone would suffer and she held herself for nothing but an 'unprofitable servant.' But she did not want God's plan to fail because of her fear. On the one side, there was only temporal harm to herself; and even this could be useful to God. On the other side, the plan of God was at stake.

Mary already realized that the sin against the Holy Spirit is the only one that always has irremediable consequences. She preferred therefore to fail in obedience to Joseph rather than to the Holy Spirit. In giving her consent, she took care first to affirm very plainly that she was the handmaiden of her Lord. This was a kind of declaration of good will. Then without further hesitation, she replied unconditionally to the request that had been made of her: "Let it be done to me according to your word."

The Holy Spirit responded to the heroism of his spouse by a new outpouring of grace. This is the moment in which he gave himself to her, bringing about the miraculous conception of Jesus. Mary's faith was then not only confirmed interiorly but also, as we have already explained, given new fullness in its objective contents, by the light which accompanied this new gift.

Then she understood that in addressing her directly, instead of passing through the intermediary of Joseph, who had responsibility for her in Jewish society, the angel was in effect announcing a new era. God was giving himself in a new way — not only with a new love, but also in a new regime. The New Covenant was being given to her along with the Incarnate Word. The Holy Spirit made her sense that the infant in her womb was to be from that moment on not only the focus but the standard of her entire life. As well as her child and spouse, he was to be her teacher, king and priest. This in turn clarified the sense of the statement that her Jesus was to be the King of Israel. The solution to her problem of conscience was thus completed; or better her peace of mind was restored by the light shed on the consent which she had given in darkness.

However, the Word who had to come to complete the revelation of the prophets by his existence in the flesh was still hidden in her womb. Although a substantial Word, he had been given in silence, as fire rather than light. Hence, it had to be through a spokesman, namely the angel, that the Heavenly Father authoritatively summoned Mary, in this profession of faith, to follow the Word in person, the Word Incarnate in place of the Synagogue. Such was, in effect, the decision asked of her.

The Spirit who dwelt within her and inspired her entire life, and the substantial Word who was about to become her teacher and master, even for her exterior life, were intimately united in a single love. This amounted to an eminent restoration of the state of original justice that had been lost by sin. Nevertheless, the Word and the Spirit remained concealed in the darkness of her faith. In coming into the world, the Substantial Light had extinguished all partial and preparatory lights by its own fire; yet it remained buried in matter itself.

This nakedness of Mary's faith made her the first in the ranks of believers. Here was no mixture of light and darkness, but the utter midnight of faith. By the same token, Mary was the first of those who must live by hope. She was a woman bearing a secret all by herself; she could not even speak of it to Joseph, her visible protector. By her act of faith, she had given up the sole visible support that God had provided to defend her from this world so alien and hostile to her.

The Visitation: The Divine Response to Mary's Anguish

Even though her anguish was now over, Mary's heart remained crucified because of Joseph. She sensed deeply that the Holy Spirit wanted her to keep silence. Moreover, she knew that she was quite incapable of explaining this event to Joseph. With her acute sense of all that was mysterious about it, she saw that it would be impossible by human words to make anyone understand it, or even admit the possibility of it, if the interior witness of the Holy Spirit were not given at the same time. She had confidence in Joseph, but this very confidence made her suffer and foresee the problems that this was going to pose for him.

Is not this the perspective in which the Visitation must be regarded if we are to perceive its hidden meaning and greatness? It occurred apparently before the angel's appearance to Joseph in a dream (Matthew 1:20). Here too, there is a mystery: Elizabeth, a humble and modest woman, with no apparent title to such priority, was given precedence over Joseph, Mary's husband. Was this not God's way of indicating the absolute sovereignty of his good pleasure? Was it not also his way of reminding the 'stronger' sex, in which the aggressive ego predominates, of God's predilection for the humble and weak?

In the hidden designs of Providence, the Visitation was above all the meeting of two little children of God in the love which had come to them through the mystery of the infants borne in their wombs. Both had a secret which they were keeping in silence. Up to this moment, Mary was the only person who knew the secret, so crucifying for her as spouse of Joseph. To a lesser degree, Elizabeth also may be said to have had a secret. She was not completely alone, but since the miraculous conception of John the Baptist, she had nothing but silence from her husband, Zachary, stricken dumb because of his moment of unbelief.

These women had been living in silence, with their unborn babies. Their faith and hope must have been heroic, when we consider that they were deprived of the support to which their need and their weakness normally entitled them. What consolation and support they must have received from this mysterious and unexpected meeting of their souls and hearts! In an instant, a profound mystical union was forged between them by the Holy Spirit himself through the infants they carried.

For Elizabeth, it was a confirmation of the angel's prophecy. But what a support it must have been for Mary, who had borne her secret in total solitude and silence. For her this must have come above all as a sign that God himself would make his secret known to Joseph at the moment fixed by his Providence. In the moment of anxiety that God had allowed to befall her, it had seemed to her reason impossible that anyone would ever be able to admit such a mystery without the benefit of her grace and the inner formation she had received. Now she knew that it was possible for Infinite Love. God was able to give someone else a kind of participation in the mystery which he had given to her in its fullness. He could enlighten the mind, and above all incline the heart, to accept such a revelation. This assured her that her painful trial would last only for a time. She had only to wait, to abide in the patience which was the fruit of her hope and especially of her love. What was possible for Elizabeth was possible for Joseph also. In his wisdom, God could find the way to make Joseph understand and admit such a mystery.

This is the moment when the *Magnificat* sprang from Mary's heart which until then had been obliged to keep its painful secret.

Joseph's New Role

How long did Joseph's trial last? It is impossible to say. In any case, he was eventually reunited with Mary through his own act of faith (Matthew 1:13-25). Now, however, in governing Mary's external life, he was no longer a representative of the Synagogue, but the representative of Jesus himself. He had become the foster father of the Holy Family, the guardian of the Child and his Mother.

From then on, there would be three to share their common life. From the moment Jesus came into the picture — really, even though hiddenly — this life had attained its perfect form, its true assimilation to the life of the three Divine Persons.

A new life was beginning for Joseph, too. It seems plausible that he was at this time initiated into a truly mystical life, by which he shared Mary's secret much more profoundly. This trial made him the child of Jesus and Mary in his life of faith and love. In the grief of her heart, Mary had given birth to him spiritually. At the beginning of her life with Joseph, she had been alone in her anguish, but her faith and heroic patience merited the interior grace given to Joseph in his dream. (For the words of the angel must have been accompanied by a very special grace, giving Joseph assurance that the angel indeed came from God, and clarifying the few mysterious words spoken [Matthew 1:20-21].) This was the moment when Mary was given finally and definitely to Joseph as his spouse. The Gospel would seem to indicate that their life together in a stable and permanent way began at this moment, sealed by the gift of the divine child entrusted to their care.

The sorrow that hung over Jesus' conception at the Annunciation contrasts mysteriously with the total, untroubled joy of his birth at Christmas. It is true of course that he was born in poverty and humility. Mary and Joseph underwent the humiliation of being refused hospitality. They felt their poverty in many different ways. But was not this very poverty the occasion of the intimacy and sweetness of the birth of the King of Kings, who came into the world, not in a palace built by human hands, but amid the poor and humble beauties of nature which had been prepared directly by Jesus' art of love? In this spirit Joseph and Mary must have taken all the circumstances of Jesus' birth as a new sign from Providence, confirming them in their state of poverty and humility. The moment chosen by God for the birth of Jesus was the very moment in which their poverty was most keenly felt.

Such an experience, however, does not detract from spiritual joy. On the contrary, religious poverty and the humiliations occasioned by it are the *cause* of spiritual joy, when Jesus gives the sweetness of his presence in the depths of the soul. The birth of Jesus, the sight of him, his *visible* presence, surely brought new intimacy into Mary and Joseph's love for God. If any clouds remained in Joseph's soul, they were now driven away for good. The joy of Mary and Joseph at Christmas was complete, because neither of them felt any more anguish. Nothing remained to oppress their common life or cause them any suffering.

So far as Mary was concerned, the angel's message to

Joseph and that to the shepherds at Bethlehem implied both a new birth for her and a definitive confirmation and consecration of her 'monastic' life with Joseph — their common life of virginity, silence, poverty and humility. At the flight into Egypt, God gave her still another assurance that this way of life was pleasing to him. It was to Joseph that the angel appeared, warning him about the danger to the Holy Family. He is the one who had to make the decision to leave their home and fly into Egypt.

Thus Mary was confirmed in her obedience to Joseph — an obedience that extended to all the external activity of their household. Jesus had not come to withdraw them from their way of life, but to plunge them more firmly into it and to give their household a resemblance to the life of the Blessed Trinity.

Part Three

Mary's Place in the Mystery of Christ

CHAPTER 10

The Public Life of Jesus Enveloped and Inspired by His Hidden Life

We have seen how the form of life which Mary and Joseph entered by their marriage can be regarded as a prototype of the religious state. This way of life was an aid and support for their pursuit of holiness; like all other human beings, they lived in dependence on their milieu.

Jesus also adopted this state of life; but in his case, it is not so easy to say what the reason was. We have seen that he is supposed to have enjoyed the beatific vision from the first moment of his conception.[25] This being the case, his human soul must have been fixed in an act of love of supreme intensity, so that there would have been no room for growth. Hence he would have had no need of anything like the religious state, which is designed to foster the perfection of Christian love. Many contemporary theologians reject this thesis, which seems to them to detract from the full humanity of Jesus. For them, the case of Jesus would not have been so radically different from that of Mary and Joseph. But whatever be the theoretical reason, Jesus did in fact adopt the lifestyle of his parents.

Even when he attained manhood, and was able to choose the kind of life best suited to the ministry the Father had given him, he chose to remain in the house of Mary and Joseph. He seems to have stayed with them far longer than was usual in those days.

The life he chose was one of silence, hiddenness and community. Externally, he was "the carpenter's son," submissive to his foster-father; Joseph was the professional artisan. The chief reality of Jesus' life was his prayer with Mary. It was a contemplative life, but one that was completely hidden.

The second part of his life was devoted to preaching, to works of mercy and, above all, to the formation of his disciples. This period lasted only a few years — about one tenth of his whole life. Furthermore, this public life was not completely separated from the hidden life, but seems to have emerged from it gradually, while remaining enveloped by it.

As an apostle, Jesus had no fixed domicile. He did not found a monastery where his disciples could stay with him. Even the Eucharist was instituted while Jesus celebrated the Pasch in the home of a stranger — a sign that he had no property of his own where he could meet with his disciples. This is all the more touching in view of the fact that the Pasch was a *family* meal. Moreover, the Eucharist was to be the sacrament of *presence* — a fact which has turned the Church into the house of God, the place where Jesus now dwells. But while on earth he had no house of his own.

But if, in his public life, the Son of Man had nowhere to lay his head, Bethany was a kind of second Nazareth for him. It was a home where he could be at ease. There he found another Mary, one like his own mother, one who knew how to sit humbly and silently at his feet listening to his word and profiting, above all interiorly, from his presence. Bethany too was a home of contemplatives. It was like a place of retreat, of that divine repose which belongs to the hidden life.

Jesus gathered disciples around himself and formed them for the ministry of preaching and teaching; but he was not the one who looked after their material sustenance. The Gospel tells us it was Judas who carried the purse. Jesus lived as a poor and humble brother with his associates; he never adopted the role of master of the household. His disciples were not simply students attending the master's lectures, nor apprentices in his ministry; they were beloved sons, friends who stayed close to a teacher they loved, like sheep around their shepherd. What they needed most of all was his presence. They learned to know his meek and humble heart by the words and actions of daily life. When Jesus called John and Andrew, they did not ask where he lectured nor where he worked, but where he dwelt; and the evangelist adds: "they spent that day with him" (John 1:38-39). This suggests that Jesus gave the apostles a sense of the hidden life long before they withdrew to the Cenacle to wait for the coming of the Holy Spirit. He wanted to alert them to the need of keeping, even in the midst of their apostolic activities, a hidden center which would be truly the source from which they would set out, and the place to which they would always retire. "Come with me by yourselves to a quiet place and get some rest," he would say to them after their laborious mission (Mark 6:31).

Thus, Jesus' hidden life was the source of his public life, or more precisely, of his public activity.[26] The hidden life was the source of inspiration for the public life and continued during it, in the form of places of retreat and of holy repose, similar to the home at Nazareth. In such locales Jesus found those souls who had a sense of the interior life and of the intimacy demanded by his love.

The Word of Jesus

Jesus came into the world to reveal the great mystery of his eternal life of love with the Father and the Holy Spirit, and to call us to participate in it as his adopted brethren; however, there is nothing in this world that can serve to represent this life of love. He goes out into the world to preach and to give men the Word of God; yet his word is not properly a public word, it always remains an interior word. Jesus does not speak on the grounds of a mandate, i.e., a mission coming from an exterior, public authority; he speaks as a Son who has received everything from his Father, whose only desire is to make his Father known. This Son is himself a substantial Word, the very Word of God.

St. Thomas holds that it would not have been fitting for Jesus to use a written word, because writing exteriorizes a word completely.[27] The spoken word is alive; it remains united with its source, from which it emerges only as a breath, whereas a written word is dead. This is why Jesus did not dictate his teaching to scribes, but confided it to his disciples (and still more to the heart of his mother). His disciples could become evangelists, committing the Gospel message to writing; yet even they were to impart the Word primarily by way of *tradition*, which is a living mode of transmission. In any case, Jesus' word was

106

the spoken word, because it was the word of the Word, who is always *Verbum spirans amorem* — the "Word that breathes love." The word uttered by Jesus was a living continuation of the eternal and substantial Word, which does not break the divine silence. It is a totally interior word; springing from love and terminating in it.

There are other nuances also that distinguish the spoken from the written word. The latter belongs most properly to society, the former to a community. The common life of mankind requires that there be a society, namely an institution which is, properly speaking, exterior and regulated by law. Law is typically a written word.

But the juridical order of society needs to be rooted in a living milieu that is a community of brothers or friends. Every community is modeled on the family. This means that it is based properly, not on justice, but on what the ancients called *pietas*. This denotes a bond that has to do, not so much with external goods and services to be rendered, as with the natural affection we ought to have for our parents, brothers and sisters. The services rendered are meant above all to manifest and develop this affection.

Thus the spoken word (which is not entirely exterior) is typically that of a brother or mother. It is also the word of the Good Shepherd, who knows his sheep by name, and knows the needs of each. In the regard of his heart, the flock is always a "little flock," not only because of his humility, but much more because of the intimacy of his love. He carries his flock, or rather each of his sheep, in his heart. He keeps it close where he can whisper to it, confiding intimate words that spring not merely from affection, but from real love.

No doubt, the word of Jesus possessed in an eminent way the values of every sort of written word. There were times when he spoke as a teacher and master defining his doctrine: "Amen, amen, I say to you. . . ." He spoke with authority, adopting this tone above all when confronted with the world of scribes and pharisees, people hard of heart and stiff-necked. But this does not seem to have been his usual manner, adopted spontaneously when he let his heart express itself. On such occasions, he preferred the tone of a father speaking to his children (or even grandchildren); or of a brother conversing with his brothers. And when he recognized someone hungry for his love, like the Samaritan woman, hc was always ready to prolong his brotherly or fatherly conversation in more intimate, heart-to-heart talks.

The word of Jesus is also that of a friend. Jesus can speak plainly (John 16:29) and with complete freedom, to those who are no longer mere servants, but friends (John 15:15). Every apostle is a "friend of the bridegroom."

The Word of the Bridegroom

This leads to still another depth in Jesus' word: it is the word of the Bridegroom. This name was given to Jesus by John the Baptist under the inspiration of the Holy Spirit (John 3:29). This is the name by which Jesus was designated, at the dawn of his apostolic ministry, to his new disciples, who were former disciples of John. In his public life, Jesus appeared as a prophet; however, it was true then as now: anyone who listens to his word, and especially one who follows his voice, like Andrew and John, discovers where it comes from and where it leads. He discovers Jesus as the Bridegroom.

This term indicates what is most proper to the word of Jesus, and what distinguishes it from the word of the prophets, including John himself, the last of the prophets. Jesus is not just the "friend of the bridegroom"; he is the Bridegroom. John's word was one of repentance; Jesus' word was first and chiefly one of love — that is why the world does not receive it. Since the fall of our first parents, this kind of word has been practically unknown to mankind. The word of the bridegroom or spouse, in the deepest sense, is no longer uttered. Man still has a dim sense of what it should be, and makes clumsy (and indeed precious) efforts at it; but in fact, his word is more that of a friend and brother than of a true bridegroom. It can take on as many nuances as there are diverse forms of friendship; but in the last analysis, the language of friendship is proportioned to community and to the common life. That of a bridegroom, on the contrary, is solely for the bride. It is incommensurable with the exigencies of community discourse. It needs silence in order to be heard. If it requires a common life, it is that of silence, which is not the life of the human community.

The word of Jesus is, therefore, inseparable from his hidden life — the life he led with Mary at Nazareth, his only true abode. There he was truly the bridegroom — the one who has the bride.

John the Baptist, the "friend of the bridegroom" (John 3:29), had been acquainted with Jesus during Jesus' hidden life. From a distance he had glimpsed something of the life of Jesus and his mother; but John himself did not know who Jesus was (John 1:33). He had been able to live in a certain exterior promixity to Jesus, to be closely related to him, even to have been sanctified by him in an exceptional way before being born; and yet not know him, not know his true name. John may have regarded Jesus as a teacher or prophet but not as the Bridegroom. This is the great lesson that John the Baptist gives us: the prophets were indeed friends of Jesus; they received the grace to proclaim him to all the world or to the community of the faithful, by a word that was either public or familial, but they did not receive that grace which was the privilege of the Immaculate Virgin. She alone was able to have a fully intimate knowledge of Jesus because she alone had received the Holy Spirit in fullness.

At Jesus' baptism, John the Baptist also was filled with the Holy Spirit and then began to know who Jesus was. John was destined to die soon afterwards as a martyr, and God seems to have prepared him for this by an exceptional grace. The fullness of the Holy Spirit would not be given to the apostles until Pentecost; but John, who witnessed the Spirit descending and resting upon Jesus, and who bore witness that Jesus would baptize with the Holy Spirit (John 1:32-33), seems to have experienced something of the action of the Holy Spirit already. No doubt the light given to him was still incomplete; for from his prison cell, he was to send messengers asking, "Are you the one who was to come, or should we expect someone else?" (Matthew 11:3). Nevertheless, it was he who gave Jesus the mysteriously prophetic title "Lamb of God" (John 1:29, 36), and who also called him the bridegroom (John 3:29). There were things about Jesus that John the Evangelist would not learn until much later as a disciple of Mary and the Holy Spirit, but which John the Baptist seems to have perceived at the outset of Jesus' ministry. And in his case also, it may have been due to the fact he was Mary's child, the child of her tears (not those of her Compassion but those of the Annunciation). This is what gave him a certain right of entrée into the intimacy of Jesus' hidden life.

The word of Jesus arose out of the silence of love and found its fulfillment in silence. In the Blessed Trinity the Word abides eternally in the Father; it is in no way exterior. The *Logos* is a word which terminates in love. Jesus' mission on earth was indeed a visible mission, but this did not make it solely an exterior and public mission. The visible mission was subordinate to and inseparable from an invisible mission. The Holy Spirit, dwelling in Jesus fully from the moment of the Annunciation, inspired all that he said. Jesus' visible mission had as its purpose to prepare souls to receive the Holy Spirit: "It is good for you that I go, because if I do not go, the Paraclete will not come to you; but if I go, I will send him to you. . ." (John 16:7, RSV). It is the Paraclete who will teach from within all that Jesus has said in words (John 16:13f). No longer does Jesus speak in parables; he speaks truth (John 16:25, 29). But this truth is one of love and life; it cannot be understood fully and according to the mind of Jesus except by the light and the loving presence of the Holy Spirit. He has to dwell in us.

Thus, the word of Jesus is a word of silence and love. It always has to be enveloped in love, and cannot subsist outside it. His word springs from the silence of the hidden life and needs to terminate in the silence of prayer.

The Word of Jesus and the Cross

Jesus' word of love is closely connected with the cross. It leads to the cross and gives us a thirst for the cross, for it makes us understand that here below every word is limited in its substance and incapable of being a sign of the substantial word which is the Word of God. The *Verbum spirans amorem* calls for some other sign to complete the spoken word. The latter is a way leading to a sign much more perfect than itself — the cross, the only visible sign of love here below that is complete.

The Passion was the culmination of Jesus' preaching. It was not just the martyrdom of a prophet, it was a free, voluntary sacrifice, the sacrifice of love by the Bridegroom offering his own body for his bride as a victim of love. The cross represents and proclaims for sinners and for the whole world the superabundant love of God. Mary had received this love at the Annunciation, at the dawn of the new hidden life brought about by the tiny infant whom she did not yet see, but who was already for her a being of fire.

Jesus' word of love sprang from his hidden life and was like an attempt to share with his brothers this life of love that he had been living in a completely hidden manner with Mary. The words of the Good Shepherd in his preaching were echoes of all the intimate words spoken by Jesus to Mary during the thirty years of their hidden life. But no preaching, not even that of Jesus himself, could express or make us understand the mystery of infinite Love, the hidden, silent intimacy that can exist here below between Jesus and his "little ones," especially Mary, the Queen of Love and Mother of these little ones. Mary is the only one who fully knew the infant Jesus, and who enjoyed that intimate relationship with him of which his littleness was the sign. She alone had the dispositions necessary to receive and keep in her virginal heart the word of love spoken by the Divine Spouse. Fallen man has lost the sense of intimacy and littleness. There was no other way for Jesus to make us understand the nature of his love than by the sacrifice of the cross. Mere words could not express it.

For us sinners, the cross stands between the word of Jesus and the intimacy of the hidden life. After instructing us by his word, in its various forms, and perhaps after asking us to share his word with others, Jesus can give us no greater grace than that of asking us to share his Passion. In the perspective of love, sacrifice is more precious than any service. Greatness and growth mean nothing for love except insofar as they offer more matter for sacrifice. And only after our ego has been put to death through participation in his agony and Passion, can Jesus bring us into the intimacy of his hidden life.

CHAPTER 11

The Unique Mode of Mary's Sanctification

The hidden life of Jesus with Mary is the royal moment in the life of the King of Love. In order to see this, we must consider the unique and privileged mode of Mary's sanctification, and of her union with her beloved Son in the Holy Spirit. This is the great mystery of her life, which we must approach with humility, but also with the boldness that is the right of children. We will see that matter plays an essential role in these two complementary mysteries, and this will give us some inkling of the meaning of matter and, indeed, of the whole material universe.

For Sinners: The Cross and the Sacraments

Like his public life and his preaching, the cross of Jesus is a mystery which must be viewed in the light of his hidden life in order to be understood. The hidden life and the cross are like two signs invented by Divine Wisdom to represent Infinite Love, for love implies both intimate union and sacrificial gift. The cross is the sign chosen for sinners, the hidden life the sign for Mary.

Of course, the Blessed Virgin also shared in the cross of Jesus, and even more profoundly than anyone else, precisely because of her intimate relationship with him in his hidden life, and because she was Mother of the Faithful. Nevertheless, the hidden life in its full, substantial reality was the sign chosen specially for her, the one most proportioned to her virginal love. It was in the hidden life that Jesus sanctified Mary as the Immaculate One. She is the only person ever to have had a truly intimate and in fact interior contact with the adorable body of Jesus, the unique instrument of divine grace.

All of us, to be saved, have to have contact with his body, which is the efficacious sign bringing us into the Trinitarian life of love. However, we sinners have this contact only by means of the sacraments, particularly the

Eucharist. The very meaning of the sacraments requires physical contact and, in the Eucharist, there is not only external contact, but eating and drinking: "Unless you eat the flesh of the Son of Man, and drink his blood you have no life in you" (John 6:53). Through the Eucharist, the priestly prayer of Jesus that all may become perfectly one (John 17:23) is fulfilled. The Eucharist is the sign of both the real body of Jesus and his mystical body. By it we are led to the Father and united with God, and in God we are united with our brothers. Eucharistic Communion, with the realistic sign at which so many of his hearers were scandalized when Jesus preached about the Bread of Life, recalls the sign given to Mary on the day of the Annunciation: that of the infant Jesus physically present within her. In the Eucharist too, the mystery of the infinitely little reappears.

The sacraments, by which sinners are sanctified, are basically signs of the Passion, streams of living waters flowing from the pierced side of Jesus. It is hard to say what role they played in Mary's life. Although she was present on Calvary, she was not at the Last Supper. This may be an indication that she did not need the sacraments, not even the Eucharist. Through the grace of divine motherhood, she was sanctified in a unique way, directly and totally, by a substantial contact with Jesus. (This would seem to be also the profound rationale for her Assumption.)

After Jesus' death, she presumably received Communion from St. John and took part in the sacramental sacrifice which he offered; but this could have been more for the sake of John and ourselves than for her. She embraced our conditions of life to the fullest possible degree in order to help us better. Being Immaculate, *de jure* she ought not to have remained on earth after Jesus' death. Her love drew her so powerfully toward Jesus, that a special, almost miraculous grace of strength was required to permit her to remain here. She did so in fulfillment of her Son's last wish, which he indicated by entrusting St. John to her as he hung from the cross.

On the other hand, since she *did* remain here below, exercising her motherhood of mercy in regard to sinners,

114

perhaps she really did have need of the Eucharist. This sacrament is the sign of Jesus, not only in the mystery of his Passion, but also in his victory; it is the sign of the glorified body in which he will come on the last day. Mary had no direct contact with Jesus' glorified body. This would not seem to have been possible except by a miracle, since her body was still liable to suffering and death. Thus she may have needed the Eucharist as the sacrament and sign of Jesus' glorious body and of the relations all are called to have with him in glory. Perhaps we should say that the Eucharist was given *above all for her* as a viaticum in a very literal sense, to enable her to stay a while longer in this exile. Was it not the pledge of her hope and the Bread of Life preparing her for the Assumption?

Sinners, at any rate, are sanctified by the sacraments — external rites, professions of faith which we make as members of a community of believers. Certainly, they give us grace and enable us to have a close personal union with Jesus; this is what differentiates them from mere liturgical ceremonies.[28] The latter are performed in the name of the Church, whereas the sacraments are the very acts of Jesus reenacted for us in the sacramental mode. Their power is that of Jesus himself, transmitted instrumentally and efficaciously by them. But insofar as they are signs and external rites in the form of a profession of faith, the sacraments pertain to public worship and are directly proportioned to the community of believers.

Mary Sanctified by Direct Contact with Jesus

Mary, however, was sanctified in the mode proper to the Spouse and Queen by a direct and total contact with her King. Not only had she been preserved from sin, she had been singled out and set apart from the entire community of men and angels to be united directly to the physical body of the Son of God through her motherhood. This defines the sense in which she was Bride and Queen. Even though the physical bond of motherhood between her and Jesus was essentially temporary and had to disappear, the mysterious yet very real love

115

relationship which the Holy Spirit had thereby established remains forever. Foreseen and determined in
Mary's predestination, it was actualized gradually and
progressively during the years between the Annunciation
and the Assumption. In the hidden life at Nazareth,
Jesus loved his mother with a tenderness no other
human love has ever attained. And when the time came
for her to be glorified as queen, he did not wait until his
entire people had attained its fullness and was ready for
the resurrection, but gave her the fullness of glory at
once, in body as well as in soul.

The Meaning of Mary's Hidden Life

The period which elapsed between Mary's first contact
with Jesus in his conception and her final union with
him in glory, seems to have been designed by God to
bring out all the virtualities latent in the divine motherhood as intended by him. This would seem to be the
basic reason for, or rather the very essence of, Mary's
hidden life.

The Annunciation had been a veritable new birth for
her. We have seen how it blotted out, in a sense, all the
light she had inherited from the sacred tradition of her
people. In its place, she received in her bosom the Substantial Light — the very Word of God, foretold and
prefigured by all the created symbols and lights of the
Old Testament. The act of faith required of her at that
moment indicates that God was demanding a kind of
break with her Hebrew past, so that she might live solely
with her little one, and be totally and exclusively a disciple in his school. Later he would show her what she
was to keep from the old economy and what had been
suppressed by his coming. He wanted her to actualize
fully the new littleness which he was introducing into
creation, an intuition of which was given to her in a flash
of fire, while the grace for it was given in a stable, permanent way with her loving motherhood.

Soon afterwards Joseph had been restored to her, enabling her to plunge still more deeply into that hidden life
as the "mother of fair love," consecrated entirely to her
divine child. Mary began a completely new life with him,

116

not only at his birth, but already at the moment of his conception.

Her grace of being immaculate must have entailed capacities of littleness and inwardness which remained latent until this moment when they could germinate under the direct interior influence of the Sun of Justice himself. The virginal fountainhead conferred on Mary at her conception now proved to contain depths still unplumbed. She discovered the disparity between her virginal love which had begun in the form of an infant's love for its mother, and her grace of being immaculate which, though given at her conception, was properly the grace of the Mother of God.

Led by Jesus and the Holy Spirit, she began to draw upon this fountainhead which until then had remained hidden and unknown to her. In a union of love with her unborn child, she lived the mysterious life which he led as an infant in her womb. By the same token she also lived his life as Son in the bosom of the Father. Mary was completely hidden in her little one, stripped of everything, in the total surrender which he asked of her from the moment he began to exist within her. Physically, Jesus was inside of Mary; mystically, Mary was carried and enveloped by Jesus.

Mary's Body and the Mystery of Light

Under the influence of the fire of love burning in the heart of her little child, who lived in the vision of God, Mary's virginal and immaculate body also underwent a marvelous transformation. Let us try to understand something of it.

The bodies of the saints in glory will be made luminous and radiant by the love which arises in them from the beatific vision. This love will permeate the body completely and transform it. It is not only the intellect and will which can be supernaturalized and divinized by love, but also the body, thanks to the matter of which it is composed, and which is in no way an obstacle to its sanctification.

Mary's body on earth was not glorified like that of the saints in glory. It did not have a luminosity visible to the

117

human eye. The glow of light which comes in the beatific vision from the body's being irradiated, or rather permeated, with love, was not yet hers. Even Jesus' own body (except, of course, at the Transfiguration) did not reflect the rays of light coming from the Sun of Justice (although it was completely penetrated by invisible rays of 'fire').

Jesus' body, and especially his heart, were truly the instrument of Infinite Love — not an inert instrument, but one that was alive and loving, wholly permeated with Divine Love, supernaturalized and divinized, even while remaining subject to the conditions of a passible body. (This touches on the mystery of the Sacred Heart, the meek and humble heart of Jesus.)

So likewise Mary's human body was completely penetrated by the invisible rays of love, which were perfectly compatible with the 'darkness' inherent in matter. The immense love contained in the body of Jesus was transmitted to her passible body, not as rays of light, but as invisible rays of interiority, warmth and fire. Her body may not have been as luminous as those of Adam and Eve in the state of original justice, but it was in a higher state as regards love.

The light of the world in which we live is only a pale reflection of the Substantial Light of the Divinity. If the former consists, not only of visible rays, but also, and even more importantly, of invisible ones, which penetrate into bodies, imparting a mysterious warmth and energy to them, what must be the case of the Substantial Light itself, which is properly an interior light?

To the eye of faith, physical light is an image of the Substantial Light more by its invisible rays than by the visible ones. In matters of faith, there is always one aspect that is dark and mysterious and another that is luminous. The dark aspect is the substance of the mystery; it remains dark even in mystical union. The luminous aspect is nothing but an aura meant to lead us to the substance.

From a slightly different point of view, we can say that physical light has two aspects, or that it is operative on two planes. On the one hand, there is what may be called the exterior or surface plane. Light illumines objects, their contours and lines. This is what the artist exploits and captures in his paintings (in which, however, it becomes abstract and frozen). This is what reason seeks to utilize, because by means of it we get to know the form and limits of things.

On the other hand, light has an aspect of inwardness and warmth, whereby it corresponds with matter more than with form. Because of this aspect, light does not merely glance off the surface of things; it touches them inwardly. The difference between natural and artificial light consists largely in this inwardness and warmth of invisible radiation touching, penetrating and enveloping our bodies.[29] Natural light, being a reflection of God, has a *restful* effect on our sensibility which it elevates and disposes in a way naturally favorable to the supernatural life. Artificial light, on the contrary, *enervates*; it excites the senses and imagination, it violates and even destroys the delicacy of that deeper, more spiritual sensibility in us, which is like matter for the Holy Spirit's work.

The gifts of the Holy Spirit orient us toward the inward aspect of light by drawing us into recollection in a direction quite opposite to that of the imagination and reason. This is the direction of the heart, which longs to go more deeply, or rather allows itself to be drawn, toward the hidden, substantial source of light. It does not attach itself to light out of love for the light itself, but sees light as a reflection of, and a way to, the warmth of love.

CHAPTER 12

The Role of Matter in the Suffering of Jesus and the Sanctification of Mary

The contact established between Jesus and Mary at the Annunciation gives us a hint of the immense and mysterious role which matter plays in the Incarnation of Jesus and the sanctification of his mother. We will try to probe this mystery more deeply by seeing, first, how matter makes suffering possible and how suffering, rather than injuring love, can nourish it. Then (in chapter 13) we will examine the union between Jesus and Mary which began at the Annunciation and continued to develop until their ultimate heavenly union in the Assumption.

Matter, Suffering and Love

From a theological point of view, there are two mysteries in the Incarnation. The first is the very fact of a divine person assuming a human nature; this mystery remains even after Jesus has been glorified. Secondly, there is the sorrow and pain which the Son of God endured on earth.

The fact that Jesus' body was capable of suffering made it possible for him to die the violent death of the cross. However, it is very important here to distinguish between the simple, natural capacity of the human body for physical suffering, and a kind of moral or spiritual suffering which closes a person in on himself. Although both result, directly or indirectly, from original sin, the latter is an obstacle to love and inhibits its development, whereas the former can contribute to its growth. We saw in chapter 5 that there is a kind of suffering that perfects the soul's profound sensibility, thereby making it more receptive to the Holy Spirit. Concupiscence, on the contrary, i.e., desire that is impetuous and ill-regulated, exercises the aggressive ego. Even the pleasure-lover is turned back upon himself. His attitude, springing from the ego and imagination, fastens on the pleasure and takes possession of it for the ego. In love, on the contrary, there is the passivity of surrendering to God while forgetting about oneself.

Adam and Eve before the fall were immune to suffering, but their love did not equal that of Jesus and Mary. This was partly because God used the capacities for suffering in the latter to subject them all the more completely to his love. By being able to suffer, their bodies provided a matter that was all the more passive and malleable to love. Only sin and its direct effects are impervious to love.

The mystical life manifests this deep affinity between suffering and love. The case of suffering and knowledge is not the same. Suffering impedes knowledge; hence the intellectual seeks to *abstract* from his sufferings. Love, however, does not abstract us from our sufferings; it pervades and transforms them. It makes use of them as a choice material, impregnating them with an ointment that imbues them with peace joining them to love. It strips them of everything deriving from the ego. The aggressive ego is rebellious and self-centered; it aggravates suffering by the activity of the imagination, jangles the nerves, etc. Love stops all this; it makes a person stay in the present by withdrawing his suffering from the influence of the ego and placing it under the influence of love, where God may, if he so please, suffuse it with his unction and his love.

In the saints' experience of suffering, two or even three moments can be distinguished clearly. At first, suffering is accepted by the will, while the sensibility and the entire body rebel against it. Later suffering is spiritualized under the influence of a deep spiritual life, which develops that 'spiritual sensibility' of which we have spoken several times. Although the more superficial and exterior sensibility is still disturbed by the suffering, there is a deeper level where all remains at peace. Finally, suffering becomes impregnated by a mystical love which sweetens it, not by making it any less acute, but by providing a divine fortitude which transforms it.

The mystery of suffering, as we find it in the saints, especially in Jesus and Mary, reveals the hidden affinities between love and the matter of which we are made. We mentioned that Jesus and Mary, because of the heightened passivity of their bodies, had a greater capacity for love than Adam and Eve had known in the state of original justice. Now it must be added that the state of Jesus and Mary also required greater love, both in order to permeate their suffering, and to enable them to stand firm against an evil world. Not that they experienced any complicity with the world — even though the possibility which made them more passive to divine love left them by the same token more vulnerable to the world and its violence. But a greater love was needed to sustain them in the divine love amid the violence of this world, which springs totally from human egotism. In fact, their love surmounted all the violence they suffered, converting it into love.

Thus, in the case of the bodily sufferings of Jesus, it can be said that a marvelous transformation occurred in his sense of touch. What was violence on the part of the torturer turned into patience — the patience of love — when it touched Jesus' body and passed into his sensibility. His body was infinitely more sensitive than ours, and the blows that struck him did not stop at superficial zones of his being as they do in us. The first zone is that of the pleasure-loving ego which focuses on the suffering and weeps; the second is the more profound zone of the aggressive ego which mobilizes all our vital forces to react, making use of the imagination and motive powers. The blows which struck Jesus, however, went directly to his heart, the source of love. It was his love that underwent them — a love that was gentle, humble and patient. Love makes us suffer all the more by allowing the suffering to reach the very depths of our being; at the same time it transforms the suffering and utilizes it in order to love still more, with a merciful love, the one who inflicted the suffering. Jesus' reaction to his torturers was not that of defense, much less a counter-offensive; it was one of divine patience, mercy and love. His response to their violence was to love his Father all the more in his very body by letting love direct all this passivity to the Father, and to love his enemies all the more, by showing them compassion and mercy.

Light and Love

We said earlier that Mary's state, while not as luminous as that of Adam and Eve before the fall, was a better one from the point of view of love. Now we must examine this point more fully.

Light is a kind of reflection of love. It is intermediate between the inner domain of love and the exterior universe, and likewise between love and reason. It keeps both the physical world and the soul itself under the radiance of love. This is precisely the role of the 'illuminative way' in spiritual growth. The light from which it is named is a reflection or radiation of love, and leads back to love. It makes it easier for the soul to remain under the influence of love amid external activities in the household or in society.

Original justice was a state of harmony. Its inner source was love, just as with Mary. However, the conditions of the body, the family and the cosmos itself were much more favorable in that state to the luminous radiation of this love.

Original justice was a state established for the entire human community, and was meant to illumine all the activities of the community. But its light was only a disposition for love; it was not Substantial Light. It was not the light of the heavenly Jerusalem, which envelops the entire body and makes it glorious. The light of original justice did not envelop, it only illumined, because it was not a substantial light. It did not invest a man totally, as the unitive life does. The latter interiorizes everything and creates, not merely harmony, but unity between light and love. Original justice was merely a light intended to lead to love, and one that was given by the inspirations of love.

In the illuminative way, there is still a distinction between the objective light of revelation and personal inspiration, which is a kind of interior light. The two are in harmony with each other, to be sure. Moreover, they are not related simply as subject and object in the case of purely theoretical knowledge. Revelation attracts, leads toward love; this is precisely how it gives light. But it still does not imply the intimate, substantial oneness of the unitive life.

The latter cannot be realized in light here below, but only in darkness. This is not a consequence of original sin; it belongs to the very mystery of that love which is the beginning of eternal life in us. This mystery seems to be bound up with the mystery of matter — not merely in its secondary conditions, which have been affected by sin, but in its primary capacity which is inaccessible even to man himself. Matter was created directly by Infinite Love, and nothing but Infinite Love seems able to actualize it fully.

Mary's Supernatural Life

In Mary, the inner source of love had to be more intense than in the state of original justice because her external conditions were less favorable — in fact, hostile, to its development. They compelled her love to turn back all the more to its divine source, instead of radiating upon the exterior milieu. They obliged Mary's life of love to develop in a more hidden way, in a way that lies more exclusively in the dimension of littleness. Hence her love was all the more interior, abiding all the more with God, and more passive in his possession. It entailed a more complete sacrifice, because it had to be stripped more completely of everything that was not love. As a result, Mary lived all the more in the mode of the unitive rather than the illuminative way.

Her state of life was by its very nature an exceptional one — the privileged state of the Queen of Love, and of one called to make up for all others. It was not a state designed for a community but for a bride. God had not called her to fulfill any social functions, or to live among his people. He had destined her for a hidden life under peculiar external conditions that permitted her to remain constantly in the presence of the Bridegroom and in intimate union with him.

Mary was perhaps less favored than Adam and Eve in

regard to knowledge, power and in general all the activities (both speculative and practical) of human reason. But this allowed all the attention of her heart, as well as all the life-forces of her being, to be reserved exclusively for the divine Bridegroom.

Thus, conditions which appear disadvantageous from the point of view of knowledge or power, turn out to be very advantageous from the point of view of love, the only viewpoint which counts for the Immaculate Virgin. In a hostile, unloving universe, Mary was compelled to be all the more united with her Divine Spouse. The palace of the queen in which the Bridegroom deigned to dwell was thereby more hidden, silent and secluded from the rest of the universe. Thereby it became all the more an "enclosed garden" and "sealed fountain." Mary loved the added poverty and weakness which this entailed. She lived in the regime of faith; her knowledge was that of her Spouse. She loved the darkness which gave her the occasion to trust in her Beloved. His strength was hers, and she loved the very weakness which made her rely on him.

In her, God realized in a single exemplar, and to an eminent degree, that which he intended to realize in a more ordinary way in all others together. His love avenged itself on the world, by requiring an additional 'littleness' of Mary — far beyond that of Adam and Eve, because Mary had to be united to the very littleness of Jesus himself.

The sin of Adam and Eve lay in choosing the way of knowledge and reason, that is, of apparent greatness and independence, in preference to the path of the wisdom that springs from love. God did not give Mary superior knowledge or strength to help her resist the world. He profited by her weakness, which made her all the more passive, to give her greater love and to keep her even more completely in the grip of his love. He wished to keep her in a hidden life, far from the world that could not understand her, in order to form her himself as his queen and bride.

CHAPTER 13

Mary in the Father's Eternal Plans

In seeking to have as profound an understanding as possible of Mary's place in the plan of God, it is necessary to ask some very basic questions about her Son's mission and predestination. Mary is only an element in the total mystery of Jesus Christ. But in dealing with things so mysterious, we cannot always proceed in a direct and logical way. We can only bring together such glimpses of the truth as are available to us, and hope by the convergence of their lights to catch a glimpse of what we seek.

Cajetan points out that God's Love is manifested on three different planes: first by the work of creation, secondly by the grace of adoption given to all who believe in Christ, finally and supremely by the grace of the Hypostatic Union, proper to Jesus Christ himself. The Incarnation is the supreme triumph of love, the glorification of Infinite Love. Jesus is the Beloved Son, in whom the Father is well pleased, as the Father himself declared at the beginning of the public ministry (Matthew 3:17) and at the Transfiguration (Matthew 17:5), which was an anticipation of the Son's glory. Jesus was the Beloved Son in whom the Father's love was made fully manifest by the Incarnation.

Manifestation of the Father's Love

Let us begin by asking about the central aim of Jesus' mission. The Father did not send his Son into the world to be glorified by anything the world had to offer him. Neither was he sent in order to be the teacher or ruler of mankind. Without a doubt, he is King of Kings and the Master and Teacher of all; but these are simple consequences of the Hypostatic Union, not its chief purpose. Even his function as High Priest of all creation is not what properly fulfilled the will of the Father or expressed the profoundest intention of the loving heart of Jesus. Jesus came into the world primarily to manifest the Father's love. This is how he sanctified the Father's name (John 17:6, 23). He manifested the Father's love by communicating it to creatures.[30]

He did this, however, on two different levels which must be carefully distinguished, even though they are closely associated and merge mysteriously into one another. One is the communication of love to mankind at large; the other is its communication to Mary. Mary was the first and principal recipient of the Infinite Love mediated through Jesus. She was the masterpiece of his love. Before all else, he came in order to form for his Father a beloved daughter in whom the Father could be well pleased. Then after her and in her likeness, the rest of the community received the blessing of Divine Love.

The Complement of Jesus' Predestination

Pius IX said that Jesus and Mary were united in a single decree of predestination.[31] To grasp this, we must recall first that it was as man, not as God, that Jesus is said to have been predestined. Predestination has to do primarily with the end for which God destines his creatures. Thus St. Paul says that Jesus was predestined to be the Son of God (Romans 1:4) — not implying that he had existed as man before becoming the Son of God, but that his human nature was created and designed to be forever the human nature of the Son of God. Everything in his humanity, all its virtualities, were to be divinized by grace — the grace of Hypostatic Union with the Divine Word. All his human capacities were used by the Word in order to be actualized to their full potential in Infinite Love.

But it was together with Mary that Jesus received this predestination. In order for him to be predestined as man in the way actually intended by God, Mary had to be predestined to be the Mother of God. Their two predestinations were intimately united in the divine love. They formed one sole predestination, because the one was inconceivable without the other. Mary was the necessary complement of Jesus' predestination.

This is the profound truth that has been manifested to us by the two most recent dogmas of the Immaculate

127

Conception and Assumption. Some great doctors of the Church in the past, such as St. Bernard and St. Thomas Aquinas, despite a deep filial devotion to Mary and an acute sense of her holiness, dared not affirm these beliefs, for fear of bringing Mary too close to Jesus.

Obviously, there is an infinite distance between Jesus and Mary so far as their being and nature are concerned. He is the natural Son of God; she is merely God's adopted daughter. She is a pure creature, a mere servant, and indeed what the Gospel calls a "useless servant" (Luke 17:10). She belongs to the least and lowest order of creatures capable of knowing God and serving him freely — the human race. But Infinite Love bridged the infinite gap between them — Jesus and Mary are one, not in nature but in love. The very darkness of Mary's faith reinforced this unity, for it meant that there was but a single light for her and Jesus. His side, facing the Beatific Vision, was luminous in glory; her side, facing the earth, was incandescent with fire.

Mary: Immaculate Virgin and Mother of God

We can approach the subject from a different angle by asking which of Jesus and Mary's various titles best express their role in the divine plan. We have already noted some of the titles accruing to Jesus in consequence of the Hypostatic Union. He is Lord of the Universe and King of Kings. He is the High Priest and Teacher of the whole world. He is the Apostle of the Father, Savior and Redeemer.

All these titles have to do with his diverse functions in regard to the created world or human society; but none of them express the essential, substantial reality of the mystery of Jesus' person. Neither do they account for the style of life he led in the world. They explain some of the things he said, and one or another aspect of his life, but not its basic pattern. (He did not live in the style of a king, priest or teacher.) Finally, it is to be noted that none of them is the name by which he preferred to designate himself. Hence, it is not in any of them that we can expect to find the proper mystery of his predestination expressed. For while predestination embraces the whole of a person's life, it refers primarily to that which is ultimate and eternal. In this sense, none of these titles can be called the name of Jesus in his predestination.

Let us ask then: What names express the external mission of the Lamb, which he continues to carry on even in the Heavenly Jerusalem? What are the names by which the blessed will glorify him throughout eternity? If Mary is linked with Jesus in a single decree of predestination, that which is ultimate in his predestination will involve her likewise. Reflection on her names, therefore, may give us a clue to the principal names of Jesus.

Mary was predestined to be the Mother of God. This was not just an earthly function, it is her eternal glory, as the definition of the Assumption confirms; for it is precisely as Mother of God that Mary is glorified in the Assumption of her body.

There is also a second title which, in the Providence of God, has been called to our attention in modern times: that of the Immaculate Conception. Four years after the definition of this dogma, Mary appeared to little Bernadette at Lourdes, saying, "I am the Immaculate Conception." Not, "I have been immaculately conceived," nor, ". . . endowed with the Immaculate Conception," but "I *am* the Immaculate Conception," as if this very grace were the definition of her being.

In truth, the Immaculate Conception is the root from which her grace and glory sprang. As the seed contains the tree, the Immaculate Conception already encompasses the Divine Maternity in the concrete form willed by the Father's love. The title *Full of grace*, with which the angel greeted Mary at the Annunciation, is nothing other than that of the Immaculate Conception under its positive aspect. In fact, it is in the form "Full of grace" that the Immaculate Conception is revealed in Scripture.

Thus we may say that *Immaculate Conception* is a name given by the Heavenly Father to this most beloved daughter of his. It is the name by which Jesus in glory loves to call her, because it indicates the love relation that unites her with him. It is the name given by the Holy Spirit to his virginal spouse. We may add that this title expresses perhaps better than any other all that was implied in that virginal love which brought forth a divine fruit under the action of the Holy Spirit. This love, the source of her entire life, was fruitful because it is passive to the action of the Holy Spirit. It kept Mary constantly under the ascendancy of the Spirit and united with him in love. This is what made it virginal, made it an image of the Holy Spirit himself, Love in person, who was her spouse.[32]

Thus, in the perspective of love (which is that of divine predestination), Mary is the Immaculate Virgin. She is the woman with whom Infinite Love was well pleased from the first instant of her conception. All the resources of her human nature were available to Love so that, in body as well as in soul, she should be nothing but a love relationship to her Beloved Son and Bridegroom.

The two great titles which best declare Mary's role in the divine plan are therefore *Mother of God* and *Immaculate Conception*. With them to help us, let us return to the examination of the titles of Jesus.

Jesus: Son of Man, Bridegroom

The name which Jesus seems to have preferred above all others is *Son of Man*. Although this title has mysterious overtones drawn from Jewish Apocalyptic,[33] we must not overlook its basic and literal meaning: "human being." The fact that Jesus lived with his disciples, not in a position of dignity, e.g., as a rabbi, but simply as a brother and a friend, reinforces the significance of this preference. At the end of his hidden life, as his public ministry was beginning, John the Baptist gave him the name of *Bridegroom*. The Son of Man is the Beloved Son of the Father, the Bridegroom.

The Synoptic Gospels insist mainly on the title *Son of Man*. They also recount various parables in which the Bridegroom figures, but it is John the Evangelist who makes the most of this term. He alone reports that, at the beginning of his public ministry, Jesus was called the Bridegroom by John the Baptist (John 3:29). In the Apocalypse, he speaks of the wedding day and the wedding feast of the Lamb (19:7, 9), whose bride is the heavenly Jerusalem (21:2, 9). Mary and the Church are seen together in this figure (cf. 12:1-17) for, in the perspective of love, they have but a single relationship to him.

The Synoptic Gospels deal mainly with the earthly life and visible mission of Jesus. In that perspective, Jesus appears as the Son of Man, with Mary as his mother. John, however, had the special function (conferred by Jesus and the Spirit), of making known the hidden and mystical aspects of Jesus' life. He illumines the mystery of Jesus and the Church by relating it to the Blessed Trinity and the divine missions. Only in such a perspective can the title of Bridegroom be understood.

The Synoptics present Jesus' preaching as a continuation and culmination of that of the prophets. Thus they put it in relationship with the purgative and illuminative life. John, by relating the Word of Jesus to the Eucharist, brings out its connection with the hidden life and its mystical values.

The role of the Son of Man can be grasped by any believer (granted, of course, that it covers further depths of mystery); but not until heaven will we see how the visible mission of the Word was that of a bridegroom. When Jesus returns, this title will be revealed fully and manifestly to the whole world. Nevertheless, St. John, the Beloved Disciple and a privileged son of Mary, was allowed to give us a certain glimpse of the mystery of the heavenly Jerusalem in his Apocalypse.

There is a certain correspondence between Jesus' titles (*Son of Man* and *Bridegroom*) and those of Mary (*Mother of God* and *Immaculate Conception*). As Jesus is the Son of Man, Mary is the Mother of God. As Jesus, the New Adam, is the Bridegroom, the New Eve, his bride, is not only the Church, but even more, the Immaculate Virgin.

Mary as the Bride of Christ

The grace of the Immaculate Conception means that Mary had the unique privilege of being encompassed by Infinite Love from the first moment of her existence. That is to say that she was the Beloved, the Bride of God, in a way that cannot be affirmed of anyone else. The Immaculate Conception oriented her radically and totally toward

God from the outset of her existence, in a love relationship which constituted her very person as seen from a dynamic and psychological point of view. The Annunciation, far from annulling this relationship, consolidated it in motherhood. Mary is the woman in whom all the resources of humanity were used in such a way that her whole being, body and soul, was nothing but a love relationship to her Son.

Similarly, Jesus, from the first moment of his existence as man, turned to her with a love that was both filial and spousal. He was united with her in the Holy Spirit from the instant he was conceived, when he began to "draw all to himself" (cf. John 12:32). The Beloved Son of the Father was also, from the first moment of his earthly existence, the beloved son of his mother, as she was his beloved mother. The Infinite Love which Jesus glorified by communicating it to creatures was directed first and above all to her. She received it in an eminent way because she was united to him in a unique love relationship.

In his human nature, Jesus contemplated the Father through the Divine Word. Hence he can be said to have remained in the bosom of the Father by his mind while, by his body, he was in the womb of Mary, communicating to her, as her Beloved Son, the love which came directly from the Father.

In giving Mary his infant body to be carried in her womb, Jesus was truly giving himself to her in love. In giving her his body, he could give his soul and divinity, just as he does now in the Eucharist; only he does this for us under the form of a sacramental sign, whereas he did it for Mary by being physically present. And although the physical function of bearing Jesus' body lasted only for a while, the love relationship which united these two persons, and made them, so to speak, interior to one another, remains forever. On Christmas Day, Jesus came forth physically from her womb. According to the bold expression of the Fathers of the Church, he came forth as a bridegroom: not with pain but in the fullness of joy. His birth did not imply any division or externalization in their love relationship; it was a perfect image of Infinite Love, realized in human matter. It was not just a remote trace, such as can be found in creation at large, but the definitive image of the Holy Spirit in his love relationship with the Father and the Son.

The Trinity Imaged in Jesus and Mary

If Jesus became a man rather than an angel, it must be that human nature offers the possibility of an image of God that angelic nature does not. By nature, the angel resembles God more closely than man does. A pure spirit's activities of intelligence and will are untrammeled by the emotions and the myriad bodily hindrances that handicap us in these activities. Hence, if we consider the universe from the standpoint of the hierarchy of natures, the angels would appear to be its culmination and its central figures.

But since the Word of God became man rather than an angel, it must be man who is at the center of the universe as in fact willed by God, with a destiny transcending the natural order. (In this connection, it is significant that in Scripture, angels always appear in the subordinate role of ministering to human beings.) However, it is not the excellence of his powers that raises man above the angels, but the fact that he offers an infinite capacity for Infinite Love to fill.

What is the profound capacity in human nature that permitted Jesus to manifest Infinite Love in a way that he could not in the angels? It is bound up with the fact that man lives in society, *not in solitude* like the angels. This fact, which is due ultimately to the matter of which man's being is composed, does not of itself make man an image of the Blessed Trinity but it does give him a possibility of representing the Trinitarian relations that pure spirits do not have. There are two human relationships in particular that are privileged images of the divine in the order of love. The first, which we have already examined, is that of the infant nursed by its mother — an image which is imperfect, incomplete and transitory. The second is that of the bride and groom; but it has been spoiled by sin, so that what we have left in the actual order of things is only a dim reflection, rather than the proper image of Divine Love originally intended. Artists working with inanimate materials may be able to represent the physical gestures of love with a certain purity of form; but the human reality has been radically disfigured by the aggressive, pleasure-seeking human ego. Nevertheless, the nuptial image remains central throughout Scripture, from Genesis through the prophets, the Song of Songs, the Gospels and Paul to the Apocalypse.

In the state of original justice, these two images, of the infant and of the spouses, were probably meant to complete each other. They would have been like two natural sacraments, inspiring and culminating the community life of brotherhood and friendship. More than any other functions in human life, these two are susceptible of being supernaturalized and divinized in their very substance by Infinite Love. Other relationships are based on particular functions; these two alone are able, under the inspiration of Infinite Love, to take two human lives in their entirety and join them together in an immediate and total relationship. In Jesus, the two figures, Son of Man and Bridegroom, are unified in a single one which is inconceivably more perfect.

While Jesus was being carried in Mary's womb, the two of them were united in love more totally than Adam and Eve would ever have been. They were in fullest truth "one flesh." The Divine Spouse came forth from Mary's womb, not to put an end to this image of the Blessed Trinity, but to perfect and confirm it. He appeared in order to reveal to her the implications of his coming for all creation; but in showing her his face, the fruit of her womb did not diminish their love relationship; rather, he gave it a new dimension.

Hence, what is brought about in each of us by the grace of adoption is typified in Jesus and Mary, and in their very humanity, by a relationship that embraces their entire being and their complete natures in uniting them to each other. In them, God exploited the infinite capacities of pure matter in such a way as to unite them in a supernatural love which embraced the entire being of each, body as well as soul, from conception onward, and related them to each other and to him. The body is not an accidental but a substantial part of the human being.

That is why the love relationship between Jesus and Mary cannot be dismissed as merely 'accidental.' Their very substance, their persons *qua* human, are in a love relationship with each other by reason of a union of love that encompasses and permeates their being.

May we not go so far as to say that Jesus and Mary fulfilled in an eminent way the intention of the Father in creating human beings as man and woman? The nuptial union of man and woman was destined to give the universe its meaning — a meaning of love. Even though, by nature, humans are only very remote likenesses of God, without much more resemblance to the divine nature that can be found among plants and animals,[34] they bore within themselves a quasi-infinite potential, a capacity available for the creative art of divine love. This potential was never realized in the offspring of Adam and Eve; but Jesus realized it in and through Mary.

Jesus and Mary in the Mystery of the Church

Jesus manifested the Father's Infinite Love, we have said, by communicating it to creatures. In this communication of love, we have distinguished two spheres: Mary and the rest of the world. Now we must reflect on the connection between them. As a first approach, we may say that, in the plans of God, the whole universe, including even the angels, forms a single kingdom or community of love, in which Jesus and Mary are king and queen. In Mary, called by a unique predilection to be his queen, the King of Kings realizes all the potential of matter as a capacity for love. She is his masterpiece, a masterpiece of love. She is a beloved daughter for the Father and a spotless bride for himself. She is not sanctified as a member of the community, but as a person in her own right, as his bride.

In the mystery of the Church, two aspects may be distinguished: 1) There is the *mystical* aspect, the aspect proper to love. A foreshadowing of the heavenly Jerusalem, it remains hidden here below, being lived in an invisible way. This aspect was highlighted by Jesus in his Last Supper discourse, which was couched entirely in terms of "children" and "beloved friends" — in other words of love relationships. 2) Then there is the *organic* aspect — that of a people, a community, the members of which have different functions for the community.

In other words, the Church is constituted by two sets of relationships: a love relationship with the mystical Bridegroom, which unifies the entire community in love, and then the whole complex of relationships of the members with one another according to their respective functions. The former is the work of love in its *unitive* aspect: the latter is inspired by love, but in the way proper to the illuminative life.

Both of these aspects have their symbol in the human body. The life and growth of the body is representative of the organic aspect. In this sense, the Church is called the Body of Christ (Romans 12:4-8; I Corinthians 12:12; Ephesians 4:11-16). The mystical aspect is represented by the human body in its love relationships, but only as realized and interpreted by Infinite Love. In this sense, the Church is called the Bride of Christ. In both cases, there is more than a mere symbol or a comparison, there is a true mystery.

God's eternal plan embraces not only our relationship with him (both in grace and in glory), but also our relationship with the community within which we are sanctified. Even though grace unites us to God directly as children and friends, we are meant to develop and mature in the bosom of the community in which he has placed us. Grace builds on nature, and it is an exigency of our nature that we belong to a community. Hence we can be said to be sanctified and glorified as members of a community, a Mystical Body.

But in the case of Jesus and Mary, their love relationship with each other is what God has first of all in view, not their function in the community. It is by this relationship above all that Jesus accomplished his mission, and that Mary was sanctified. God did not intend their relationship for the sake of the community, but for its own sake, and in reference to nothing other than Infinite Love.

They may be said to belong to the first decree of divine predestination, and the rest of the Church to a subsequent decree (if we may be allowed to indulge the weakness of our human minds by speaking thus of realities which, in God, are all one). The Bride of the Lamb is both Mary and the Church; but Mary in the first instance, and the Church secondarily. The spousal relationship of the latter is modeled on that of the former.

Jesus is the one Bridegroom both of his Queen and of his Church. The Church is not a physical person like Mary; it is a people; but the spousal love of Jesus makes it truly his body and his Bride. It has the form of the Bride only insofar as it abides in the Bridegroom's love — that very love which began at the moment of his conception, in his love relationship with Mary. Even in this respect, Mary is Mother and Queen of the Church.

Some Human Analogies

It is always difficult for us to raise our minds to the level of Infinite Love. We naturally tend to think in terms of justice. Yet, even in human affairs, and among the traces of the divine which occur in the universe, there are examples that help us gain some notion of this mystery of Mary as the unique bride and masterpiece of Jesus.

Take, for instance, the difference in attitude between an employer and a friend. The employer, who has employees related to him by a contract in justice, wants them to observe the regulations he has laid down, and perform the tasks he has assigned. One employee who does his work perfectly does not make up for the mistakes or negligence of a hundred others. Likewise, if the employees work with sentiments of affection or even friendship, this does not change their situation as it is viewed from the point of view of justice. The employer, as employer, would rather have all of his employees be conscientious, even if none of them had any affection or friendship for him, than to have a few who were zealous and devoted, along with many who were negligent. Justice necessarily looks at things quantitatively.

But in the case of friendship, and still more of love, things are quite different. A single true friend outweighs a thousand superficial ones. Quantity and number count for very little in this realm. In fact, a multitude of superficial friends would of themselves be an obstacle to deep friendship (except perhaps in the case where the love is very humble and merciful).

What matters most in friendship is a heart able to receive our most intimate secrets, and ever ready to sacrifice everything for this friendship; a heart sensitive to our thoughts, desires, aspirations and suffering, capable of understanding their finest nuances; a heart of generosity and disinterestedness that we can always count on. A large number of friends who are rather sensitive and generous, but have not the ultimate perfection, the last fine point, required by true friendship, will never replace a single one who does.

Something similar can be said about works of art. Many mediocre paintings, or even works of real talent, are not equivalent to a single masterpiece. However, quantity intervenes in the domain of art much more than in that of friendship and love. Even though one masterpiece is preferable to anything else, another work that is merely talented adds something to it — if not from a purely aesthetic point of view, at least as a possession. We would rather own both together than the masterpiece alone.

A true friend, however, is never looked upon as a possession, but as a free, reciprocated gift. He is never compared with another, so long as the attitude proper to friendship is retained. Human reason loves to make comparisons, but this is repugnant to the purity of love. Only when our friendships retain a certain underlying egotism do we calculate (consciously or unconsciously) that it is safer, for example, to have several friends, in case one or another should leave us or be taken away. A generous and disinterested heart finds the very thought of such calculations repugnant. A certain element of risk seems to belong to the very essence of love, as a witness to its trust and abandon, as well as to its disinterestedness. Of course, no merely human friendship is or ever can be purely disinterested. It is only among supernatural friendships, those formed by the Holy Spirit himself, that we find examples of perfect friendship. But even these are only feeble approximations of the unique predilection of Infinite Love for Mary, his bride.

Part Four

♣

Mary and
the Church

CHAPTER 14

The Hidden Life: Source and Summit of the Church

The Church of Jesus is not merely a pastoral office for teaching and directing. It cannot be reduced simply to the ministry of grace through preaching and sacraments. It is also the Bride of Jesus, in the image of Mary. By its most intimate prayer, and by lives that are totally sacrificed out of love, the Church is consciously the Bride of Jesus. She remains at each moment totally and directly united to the Sacred Heart of her divine Bridegroom, from which she sprang on Calvary.

The Church participates in the prerogatives of her divine Spouse as king, teacher, apostle and priest. She carries on all over the world the mission which he entrusted to her in the words, "Go and make disciples of all nations, baptizing them. . ." (Matthew 28:19). By a mandate from him, she exercises the same function which he exercised during his public life, and applies to human beings the merits which he acquired at the price of his blood.

But the public life of Jesus, or more exactly the public and apostolic *activities* of his life, remained enveloped by the hidden life. The latter inspired them and could even be called their goal, as we have already said. This hidden life, however, was a privileged domain, reserved to Mary. This life of deep silence in which every word and action remained directly and totally under the dominion of love, was very properly the intimate life of spouses.

Jesus wanted this hidden, silent life perpetuated in his Church. He willed that the Church, cleansed in his blood and redeemed at the price of his life, the Church for which he has given his body in a sacrifice of love, should also be a bride like Mary. He loved the Church as his bride. He wanted it to look to him as a bride to her spouse. He wanted it virginal and immaculate like Mary.

That is why, on Calvary, before his death, he entrusted the Church, in the person of the apostle John, to his mother.

Peter and John: The Apostolic and Contemplative Lives

The previous evening, he had given the Eucharist to all the apostles, who had previously received the mission to baptize. He had already given Peter special powers of jurisdiction and authority. Peter, the supreme pastor, was to be like a standard of measurement, which has to be unique. Later on, after first ascertaining Peter's exceptional love ("Simon, do you love me more than these?") Jesus would give him the charge, "Feed my sheep" (John 21:17). Peter had to love Jesus even to the point of martyrdom. He too had to be a good shepherd who would lay down his life for his sheep.

As he hung from the cross, just a few minutes before his death, Jesus commended his mother to the apostle John. This took place in the presence of those women who had known something of his hidden life, and who had had the courage to follow Jesus to the very end. They had won the right — a right of love — to be the loving and compassionate witnesses of his death.

Mary was given to John as a gift of love. It was not a matter of a function or a power as in the case of Peter, but truly and simply a gift of love. Likewise, it was not properly a sacrament that Jesus bestowed on the two of them: Mary at least had no need of a sacrament. The words "Woman, behold your son; ... behold your mother" (John 19:27) expressed a mystery realized for John and for us all by the will of Jesus. We are told that John took Mary into his home; Mary went to live with John.

The entire mystery of the Church, as it was conceived and intended by Jesus himself, is indicated in the way these functions and gifts were conferred on the apostles.

As St. Augustine puts it, Jesus entrusted his Church to Peter, the disciple who loved him. Peter represents active love and the devotedness of the apostolic life. But to John, the disciple whom Jesus loved, the virgin apostle, Jesus entrusted his mother. John was apparently the youngest and least of the Twelve, but Jesus had a special affection for him. He represents the contemplative life.

Having given his apostles the sacrament of his body, which represents the entire Mystical Body, at a very solemn moment of his life, the eve of his death, Jesus gave John something even dearer to his heart than the Mystical Body, and at a moment that was even more sacred. John had to be prepared for this new gift by resting his head on Jesus' heart at the Last Supper, and by witnessing the Passion, the sign of Jesus' exceeding love for men.

Jesus gave Mary to John under the title of mother. We have seen what Mary's motherhood represents in the Incarnation, and how the entire hidden life is like a development of that grace, that gift of fire bestowed on her in the person of the Divine Word himself, on the day of the Annunciation. The hidden life had been like an unfolding of the whole potential of love contained in the union between the infant Jesus, the least of all the children of men, and Mary Immaculate, the least of all the daughters of the Heavenly Father. The hidden life was nothing other than the mystery of divine motherhood experienced in all the dimensions of love.

It was a gift of love that Jesus made to John on Calvary. The circumstances of time and place, and the way Jesus expressed himself, make this evident. The great mystery that is Mary was entrusted and given in love to John for the whole Church. Among the apostles, he had the special mission of making the Church an image of Mary by a life of love. Through him and his 'progeny,' the Church was to live consciously as the immaculate bride of Jesus and at the same time the mystical mother of all the faithful.

The mission of the apostles was to preach the Gospel, with Peter as their visible head; but John had the special mission of taking Mary into his home and caring for her. At first sight he would seem to have been taking the place of Joseph. But in view of the meaning of Mary's hidden life with Jesus, and above all because it was Jesus himself who entrusted John to Mary, it would seem that John's relationship with her was completely different from that of Joseph. Jesus gave John to Mary so that she would treat him as a son, as another Jesus, as Jesus continuing his hidden life in the Church.

John became a pupil of Mary to learn the secrets of this hidden life under her maternal instruction. She taught him, not by public statements meant to be preserved in writing, but in the intimate language that is meant to be kept in the heart and shared only with the closest of friends. It was even more by her presence and her silent prayer that she imparted to him that spirituality of love and littleness that is so striking in his epistles. When he calls his disciples, "my little children" and "dearly beloved," is he not using her language, which she in turn learned from Jesus during their hidden life?

In other ages, the Church has lived more particularly the spirituality of the Synoptics or of St. Paul. Through the devotions to the Sacred Heart and to the Blessed Virgin, the Holy Spirit is causing the modern age to live more specially the spirituality of St. John. As early as the thirteenth century, St. Gertrude declared that the beating of the Sacred Heart of Jesus was reserved for the last times, as a sweet eloquence meant to rekindle the fervor of divine love in a world grown old and sluggish.[35]

The Religious Life, Prolongation of the Hidden Life

Mary experienced the mystery of the hidden life in three different states: with Joseph before the Annunciation; with Jesus (as well as Joseph for a time) after the Annunciation; and with John and the Eucharistic presence of Jesus after the Passion. In the contemplative life we are called to undergo all the various modes of this mystery, which remains one and the same in its essence, with Mary as the privileged exemplar who gives it its meaning. Without Mary, there would not even be a hidden life, for it is she who offered Jesus a poor, humble, virginal little territory where he could establish his permanent, interior abode amid a world of sinners. In the hidden life of the Church, Mary needs both humble lay brothers like Joseph and priests like John. She sees Jesus imaged in both of them.

Mary's place is central in every contemplative monastery, as a reminder that she has been given to contemplatives, as she was to John, so that in them she can remain actually and consciously present in the Church. It is also in order that she may have in the Church a special home of her own, marked with her sign, the common life of silence.

It is true that all religious orders have Mary as queen and mother. The religious life in all cases is modeled on Mary's hidden life with Jesus. The purpose of every form of religious life is to be a way of giving oneself to God alone, or of reserving oneself exclusively for him.

People enter the *active* religious life, not only to work for Jesus, but still more to follow him more closely, like the first disciples, to get to know "where he dwells," in order to live in intimate union with him. Religious life is not a *function*, it is truly a *life*. It is in his very living that the religious seeks to be like Jesus; this is why he makes the three vows which consecrate his entire life. This is why traditionally he has a monastery or at least a 'cell' — a place of silence to which he can retire.

So also Jesus, in his earthly life, willed to have only a single abode,[36] from which he went out into the world to preach and do works of mercy, and to which he returned for the repose of silent prayer. This abode was first at Nazareth, later perhaps at Bethany or some other hidden, silent place; but always it was a locale of the hidden life. There he could once again be with the Father, from whom he had received all things, and with his beloved mother, the only one to whom he could give all that he had received (since the world rejects, or accepts only grudgingly, what he offers).

Contemplatives have been placed particularly under the sign of silence. They have the sweet but awesome responsibility of being in the Church the sign of this mystery of silence which is so intimately connected with Mary's hidden life and virginal love. The absoluteness of this silence may make it one of the most difficult mortifications of their life, but it is also the sure pledge of very special interior graces of the Holy Spirit, to give them an understanding of the mystery which it signifies and, still more, to enable them to live it.

The Church: Bride of Jesus and Mystical Mother of Men

Like Mary, the Church is both bride and mother: the bride of the Lamb and the mystical mother of mankind. These two titles correspond to two love relationships arising out of a single love. They explain how the Church's motherhood has depth and intimacy on the one hand, and universality on the other.

Is it not this bridal love which constitutes the mystery of the Church? Jesus committed to the Church not only the liturgical prayer and exterior cult which perpetuates his priestly functions visibly. When he entrusted Mary to John,[37] all the silent prayer of union with God, the prayer proper to the bride, became the Church's responsibility.

This is the mystery of Jesus' priesthood. His sacerdotal functions are centered on his sacrifice which, although visible, exterior and public, was also a sacrifice of love. The matter of this sacrifice was Jesus' own body; his very life, his entire person is what is offered. The secret of his hidden life, buried deep in his heart, was laid open by the centurion's lance. All external worship in the Church needs to be inspired by and terminate in the intimate and silent prayer of love, if it is to be carried on in the spirit of Jesus. Then it is truly the prayer of the bride.

When Mary was commended to John, the hidden life of the mystics was committed to the Church's care. Buried and hidden in her, they can live in union with God and love him as little children and beloved spouses. There are immense depths of intimacy in the Church's mothering of these little ones who have been entrusted to her pastoral office and ministry in order to be protected from the world. She nourishes them with the Word of Jesus in her preaching, and still more with the Body of Jesus in the Eucharist, which they so dearly need. There are times when the apostles of Jesus have a dim notion of the graces entrusted to these souls by Jesus and the Holy Spirit, of which they themselves have no direct experience. Then their role resembles that of Joseph, protector of the Blessed Virgin, or of John, her priest.

But the Church's mystical motherhood, precisely because it is so profound, extends far beyond the direct range of preaching, teaching and the entire apostolate.

This motherhood goes farther than the Church's jurisdiction; it reaches all mankind. By being the spouse of Jesus through her hidden life, intimately united to his heart, she exercises this mystical motherhood in regard to all human beings, especially those of good will. An immense multitude of people today are beyond reach of the Church's visible action, i.e., its teaching and sacramental ministry. But if they are open to the grace of God, they become children of God even without knowing it, and the Church bears them in her bosom, although they are totally unaware of her. For the grace they have received is in fact a Christian grace. It comes to them from the heart of Jesus and Mary, from that love relationship which unites these two.

Through Jesus' ministry and Passion, this love relationship is extended to and embraces all mankind. And it is this very love relationship which constitutes the mystery of the Church as the bride of Jesus and mystical mother of mankind.

The grace received from Jesus, of a love relationship with his person, is signified visibly by the Eucharist. The latter has been entrusted by Jesus to the visible Church and to the ministry of his priests, which in turn comes under the jurisdiction of Peter. Is there not here a sign that all those people of good will, who perhaps will never come under the jurisdiction of the Church, nor be reached by its apostolate, are nevertheless borne by its prayer?

This applies not only to the official and public prayer of the Church, which is wholly centered on the Eucharist, but perhaps even more to the hidden and silent prayer of all those who, under the inspiration of the Holy Spirit and as pupils of Our Lady, live the great mystery of the hidden life of Jesus and Mary. Jesus in the Eucharist is very specially the hidden Jesus. Thus all those who are not able to hear the word of the Church are entrusted particularly to the silent, interior prayer of contemplatives. The Blessed Sacrament and the Blessed Virgin both hold a central position in contemplative monasteries in order to be a daily reminder of this fact.

We may say that the two extremities of the Church

have been entrusted in a special way to contemplatives. The silence of the contemplatives with its touch of the absolute, is most needed by two classes of people: on the one hand, the apostles of Jesus, pastors of souls who minister the Bread of Everlasting Life by the Word and the sacraments, especially the Eucharist. The Word of Jesus needs silence to give it a divine efficacy and a supernatural cutting edge. Silence is the fountainhead out of which it rises; and in order to have genuine fecundity, it needs to be enveloped and borne by silence.

On the other hand, there is the immense multitude of men and women who cannot be reached through the preaching and sacraments of the Church. They include both people of good will and sinners surrendered to a sinful, violent world that makes prisoners of their souls. Yet they have been redeemed by the blood of the Lamb and are children of Mary's tears. Only the silence of Jesus, the silence of his pierced heart, is able to touch them. These poor people have an absolute and immediate need of this silence, and of the Church of silence that prays and sacrifices itself for them.

A Time of Prayer and Sacrifice

From the Sacred Heart of Jesus, with which Mary's Immaculate Heart is completely one, there arises a double movement of love inspiring both the active and contemplative lives in the Church. This movement grows more intense as the world's own movement accelerates and becomes more likely to draw souls away from God.

On the one hand, there is a movement of mercy, leading the Church to make use of all the human sciences and technologies as instruments of the apostolate. She follows her children along all the paths they have taken (sometimes so imprudently!) in order to lead them back to the fold. In Catholic Action and the other apostolic movements of our time, we have seen the Church multiply the means of contact with her children, through whom she seeks to attain those who are out of reach of her priests.

On the other hand, the Holy Spirit seems to be urging his disciples more and more toward a life that is purely supernatural and evangelical, toward a spirituality wholly inspired by love, like that of Thérèse of Lisieux. The more the world gets involved in action and progress, thinking to find happiness therein, the more the Holy Spirit seems to ask his little ones to have recourse to the essential means, the so-called 'vertical' means: loving prayer and sacrifice, in union with Jesus our Redeemer and with the compassionate heart of Mary. Thus he leads men and women of good will to participate in the mysterious love of the hearts of Jesus and Mary.

At Lourdes and Fátima, the Blessed Virgin herself came to remind us of this hidden, interior movement of the Holy Spirit now at work in the world. "Pray and do penance," she said. These are the two essential functions entrusted by the Holy Spirit to his Immaculate Spouse, the Queen of Apostles and Prophets.

To the prophets who came before his appearance as Messiah, and to the apostles who came afterwards, Jesus entrusted the mission of the word. This word was twofold: it was a truth that both purified and illumined. These two sides of the scriptural preaching are represented by the two Johns, the Baptist and the Evangelist. The former came forth from Elizabeth's womb after it had been sanctified by Mary; the latter had his dwelling sanctified by Mary. John the Baptist, the last of the prophets, pointed Jesus out at the moment of the latter's baptism, and indicated what set Jesus apart from the prophets and apostles, when he called Jesus the bridegroom. John the Evangelist, the last of the Twelve, himself received a twofold mission. First, he was to keep Mary in his house and be formed by her. Then, thanks to this special formation, unique among the Twelve, he received at the end of his life the task of proclaiming a prophetic vision of the entire history of the Church in the perspective of war between the Woman and the Dragon (Apocalypse 12) — a view that goes back to the dawn of history (12:9). John the Baptist made ready the way for Jesus' first coming; John the Evangelist prepares us for the second coming: "The Spirit and the Bride say, 'Come!' " (Apocalypse 22:17).

The only mission the Spirit gave Mary was that of prayer and sacrifice. However, he did not ask her merely for the public prayer of psalms, hymns and external cult; nor merely to associate herself with the Temple priests for a symbolic sacrifice. A *life* of prayer was asked of her. Her mission was to establish in the world a poor and humble home where the hidden life could be led, a common life of silence and sacrifice. In the midst of this world of sin and sinners, it would be a privileged terrain where the Holy Spirit could abide and give us Jesus. It would be an oasis with a spring of fresh water springing up within it. This spring is Mary's Immaculate Heart, as she reminded us at Lourdes and Fátima. It was in her Immaculate Heart, in her virginal body, that the Holy Spirit produced his masterpiece, which the wisdom of the Father had in view from all eternity, even before the creation of angels and men.

Mary is the one who had to make the final preparation for the coming of the Messiah. It was he who would give the universe its true goal, who is in his own person the goal which unifies the universe and brings it to consummation by leading it back to the Father, the Unique Source of all his words and actions. Thus Mary was situated at the center of the world, and of its history. It was in her very body, on the day of the Annunciation, that the principle of the world's unity was provided by the conception of Jesus. Mary has likewise been called by the Holy Spirit to complete the purifying and illuminating work of that Word which, while inspired by God, remains nevertheless very human. This she does through a love and unity which the Spirit himself achieves in a life of silence and sacrifice.

At Lourdes, the revelation of Mary's name was linked with the two summonses to prayer and penance, which Mary gave especially for our time. She wanted Lourdes, as a place of prayer, to be under the sign of the Immaculate Conception. This is the doctrinal foundation which explains the meaning of these two practical charges, and reveals their great depth and wide range. They recall to us the mystery of the hidden life. Mary comes to remind us that this mystery is perpetuated in the Church where, according to the plans of eternal wisdom, it should grow ever more and more intense. The movement of history is causing the universe to develop in external dimensions, carrying human beings away from God. At the same time, however, the Sacred Heart of Jesus and the inspiration of the Holy Spirit are drawing the Mystical Body in the opposite direction, to the Father in the invisible dimension of littleness and intimacy, just as they drew Mary to union with God in body as well as in soul.

It may also be that the Blessed Mother is warning her children — those who have complete confidence in her, who have made themselves totally her pupils, and are able to interpret the delicate suggestions emanating from her heart, that the coming of Jesus is now very close. The present age would then appear as the great moment of prayer and penance in the history of humanity, the advent season for the Church, like the advent which Mary passed prior to the first coming of the Lord. It is also no doubt the time for social action and lay apostolate, but of prayer and penance even more, as Mary has insisted in all her recent apparitions.

The Wisdom of Love

In revealing her name and the two chief activities of her hidden life, as she did at Lourdes, the Immaculate Virgin calls us back to the wisdom of the Holy Spirit, which is also her wisdom, the true wisdom which directs the universe and leads it toward its only authentic end. She calls us back to the two great works inspired by this wisdom of love, the only works that played a decisive role in preparing for the Annunciation, the crucial moment in the history of the world. She reminds us that it is the very same wisdom, and the same Spirit of God, which direct the world today; and that the new religion established by her Son gives even greater place to these two works of prayer and sacrifice. She seems to have come at a decisive moment in history to remind us that it is her privileged children — the poor and the little ones — who are to hasten the return of Jesus by their prayer and sacrifice.

This is part of the everlasting war between the Woman and the Dragon, between the wisdom of love and the wisdom of the world. The latter reflects the world's lusts and illusions. Satan hides his artifices today under the seductive cover of science and technology. He seeks to make us forget true wisdom and the duty of prayer and sacrifice required by it. His wisdom is based on human discoveries and on a certain movement of history which undoubtedly contains some measure of historical truth, but which goes contrary to the profound inspiration of the Holy Spirit.

Mary does not want her little ones to be seduced by the artifices and illusions of a perverse and deceitful world. The world wants them to believe that men finally possess all the resources of knowledge and power needed for a radical transformation of both the physical universe and the psychological depths of man. Jesus warned us that the world would reject his word because of its false wisdom. He thanked his Father for having revealed to little ones and to the poor the secrets of the true wisdom of love which are hidden from the great and from the wise of this world (Matthew 11:25).

By the grace of her Immaculate Conception, Mary is the queen and mother of those who are little and poor, because she is the least of all. Her wisdom consisted simply in being able on the day of the Annunciation, to recognize him who was infinitely smaller than she: the tiny Jesus conceived in her womb by the Holy Spirit.

CHAPTER 15

Mary's Spiritual History and the Meaning of the Universe

In conclusion, we will review the chief stages of Mary's spiritual growth in order to determine finally the secrets of that wisdom of love which is opposed to the wisdom of the world in the way that love and the ego are radically opposed to each other.

The first period of her life extended from her birth to the Annunciation. Her spiritual life originated in that initial love which she, as an infant, had for her Heavenly Father. The education and instruction in faith and hope which she received plunged her all the more deeply into this love. She learned from her fathers, the patriarchs and prophets; but the Holy Spirit, acting within, unified, synthesized and illumined their teaching, to prepare her for the Annunciation. Mary lived always in the present moment and as a pupil in the interior school of the Holy Spirit. Her faith underwent development; but this was intended entirely for the sake of her virginal love, which it caused to grow in littleness and intimacy.

The first period of growth culminated in that sacrifice of love which was the consecration of her virginal body by her vow, and by the Holy Spirit's response at the Annunciation. This implied a total sacrifice of her previous way of life — her faith, her poverty of spirit, the magnanimous humility of her hope and even her external status. For this sacrifice she received the Sun of Justice, Substantial Light, in the darkness of faith and under the sign of a new fire. In other words, the first phase of growth terminated in a sacrifice of light and life, a sacrifice which was offered by Love in a blaze of fire.

The Second Phase of Mary's Life: The Presence of Jesus

The Annunciation began the second phase of Mary's life, implying a new birth, new growth and a new sacrifice. It also involved a new development of her faith; only now her teachers were not the elders but the Holy

Spirit and the Divine Word himself. For Mary the 'visible mission' of the Word began at the Annunciation.

Although not yet visible to her eyes Jesus was in contact with her body intimately and substantially by a touch of love, as the infant borne in her womb. This tiny infant revealed to her the great mystery of her virginal love and of the involvement in it of her own body — the body of a mother and bride, in short, the body of a woman. This was brought about by the Holy Spirit, who overshadowed the two of them, and united them by his love.

After his birth, Jesus supernaturalized and divinized Mary's external senses: her touch, sight and hearing. His physical body was the instrument of her sanctification, which it brought about directly and totally. For nine months, his body had been united with hers interiorly and in love. Now that he had come forth, he remained united with her in the light of love — that hidden, interior light which was realized for Mary as for no other creature. By it the two of them remained interior to each other, encompassing each other in a relationship modeled on that of the Divine Persons.

During the first phase of Mary's life, through the teachings of Hebrew tradition, the Holy Spirit had given her a sense of the meaning of creation. But even though her virginal love had an incomparably delicate sensitivity to the traces of God in creatures, nowhere in the world did she find a being in harmony with the presentiments of her love. In the entire physical universe there was not a creature capable of being a true sign of love for her, and endowed with the only kind of beauty which could satisfy her. Mary, the modest virgin, had never fixed her gaze on any creature, because she returned perpetually into that hidden, interior cell inhabited by the Spirit of God. But now the infant Jesus was there as the visible sign needed by her virginal love, one more than adequate for it. Each time she contemplated him, her heart was attracted, inflamed and plunged into recollection.

Mary Educated by Jesus

By her baby's attitudes toward her, by the first steps he took, and especially by the way he learned human language from her, by the meaning he gave to each new word she spoke to him, Jesus, the Word, reeducated his mother. Mary had become the disciple of one much littler than herself, and she learned infinitely more from him than from any other source. The way he received each word was a lesson for her and an education in love. There were words that Jesus loved, that he used over and over, and others that he never once pronounced. Up until then, Mary had been very silent and had spoken little with others; now she developed her vocabulary together with Jesus. She learned her mother tongue from him; he taught her how to love. Everything in Jesus' life contributed to the human education of his mother. Before, Mary had been just a 'soul,' i.e., a wholly interior person who paid little attention to the trivia of human life or to everyday experience. She was still virgin matter, ready to be shaped for the first time by her own Son, who was in truth her Spouse.

When he became an adolescent, Jesus led Mary to understand the meaning of the universe in function of the love relationship between their immaculate persons. The story of Genesis took on an entirely new sense for her. Because of his infused knowledge, and by means of the texts of Scripture, Jesus was able to reveal to her the sense of the development of the universe and of his story. He made her understand the central and unique place of the Annunciation in it. But this incomparable teacher always remained a teacher of love. With Mary, he could always speak as a spouse, in the language of love. He taught her only what was of use for love. This was the one thing necessary in his eyes, the only thing that had eternal value. He did not form Mary for the apostolate, but solely for the life of love.

Mary, for her part, received this instruction, not in her imagination or memory, but in her heart. It was with her heart that she listened, and what she learned took hold in her heart alone, leaving her imagination and memory empty and poor. She did not strive to retain what she learned by means of a reflex attitude; the teacher of all teachers was her spouse, he belonged to her, he was *present.* He was Substantial Light for her. She loved her situation of having no knowledge of her own, of receiving everything from him; she was glad to maintain the attitude of a bride: trustful, docile, possessing nothing by herself. As a result, the treasures of wisdom and knowledge which Jesus imparted to her simply united her to him all the more firmly, and by no other bonds than those of love. She remained poor in spirit even as regards her mind, because she did not receive Jesus' teaching as rational wisdom but as the wisdom of love, and she received it in the manner of a little one who always needs the actual presence of the teacher, and even an affectionate union with the teacher, in order to take in instruction. Thus all the extraordinary growth of the thirty years of hidden life and of her three years as servant and disciple of Jesus the Apostle, had left Mary still poor in spirit, and had plunged her deeper and deeper into her littleness.

Jesus: The Focal Point of Her Life

For Mary, the entire external world was unified and interiorized in Jesus. He was the only visible object that corresponded adequately to the state of her grace, which was that of the unitive way. For her loving gaze, Jesus was not an object of philosophical or aesthetic contemplation (it is repugnant even to write such a thing when speaking of Mary). Jesus was the Wisdom, the Reality, given to her by the Father and the Holy Spirit. He was the 'Real Presence' of God for her; he was the Bridegroom. For her, he was not an 'exterior reality,' he was the person with whom she was joined in a love relationship, in soul as in body, interiorly and exteriorly. Everything was unified for her in and by love.

Moreover, she never allowed her mind or imagination to isolate any particular aspect of Jesus; she remained always in that attitude of love for her bridegroom which was the virginal spring from which her whole life flowed. He gave her a new sense of beauty. He was the sole masterpiece of Divine Wisdom in which she could take delight. Looking at Jesus, speaking with him, and above all listening to him, but also praying in silence and by herself, were all acts of the one same attitude of love, which brought her back constantly to Jesus, the Jesus

155

with whom she was one. Similarly, it was not in memory or imagination that she encountered him, but in her heart, whether the encounter occurred in silence and solitude, or in physical presence.

In Mary we see how the external senses themselves can be the direct instruments of love, far more than the interior senses of imagination and memory, or even than reason itself,[38] for a soul that is filled with love and lives with the Incarnate Word.

The hidden life of Jesus and Mary enables us to understand something that Mary was given to understand by the simple presence of Jesus, namely, how the physical universe itself has been arranged by an art of love for the life of love. The divine artist has disposed everything in this perspective which is the perspective of wisdom, totally different from the perspectives of science and technology.[39] Mary's universe was not the three-dimensional universe conceived by imagination and reason. Her universe had a fourth dimension: that of love, intimacy and littleness. This was the crucial dimension for that Sinless One who had no ego, whose entire existence was simply a relationship to her Beloved.

A Universe of Light

Her universe was indeed one of light, but this light could be seen existentially only in love. In the perspective of Divine Wisdom, light seems to have been created for two purposes, or with two different levels of meaning. In the illuminative way, created light is seen as leading us to a love that is invisible; the light itself should not retain our attention. But in the unitive way, and hence as Mary saw it, created light is viewed in the perspective of Substantial Light, which now dwells in the earthly body of Jesus. In this perspective, there is a kind of proportion between Substantial Light and created light. The former needed the latter in order to make itself present to Mary's eyes. The latter then ceased to be merely a distant likeness of the former. The human body of Jesus gave it a presence. Light itself was put in a new perspective, a perspective of love. It was no longer to be considered simply as light.

Thus the hidden life of Jesus and Mary makes us see how human imagination and reason have abstracted a quantified universe from the beneficent influence and radiance of light. Light is meant to keep the created universe in actual continuity with love, and thereby unify it for us. When this is the case, the universe is not a mere space, but a milieu with a certain note of warmth and intimacy. Human science concerns itself with the quantitative aspect of things, which is almost the direct opposite of way of Incarnate Wisdom. The physical presence of Jesus meant that, for Mary, light was not merely a radiation of love, but the very presence of love. It was a foretaste of the heavenly Jerusalem, revealing how we can prepare the universe for its true destiny. By the same token, when Jesus was no longer there to illumine things by his presence, the world lost all its color for Mary.

The Third Phase: Compassion

Thus, the second phase of Mary's life also terminated in a sacrifice — the supreme sacrifice. In offering Jesus to his Father, Mary offered up her entire universe. Jesus had been the one who enabled her to grasp the universe. His words of love and his presence shed light on the history of the world, and on its actual condition. He had not instructed her by a written word which could be kept after his death, nor even by a spoken word that would remain engraved on the memory, but by that word of love which requires presence, because it is kept in the heart and in the darkness and silence of love. Hence the death of Jesus is truly a total sacrifice for Mary. It stripped her of everything. Jesus was her entire world — the world of her senses, and even the world of reason (for in Mary, reason was only an auxiliary to love). Now Jesus required of her the sacrifice of that body and that presence which were her entire life and light. The Immaculate Virgin had been nothing but a relationship of love to her Beloved, and now he was being taken away, leaving her more destitute and humble than ever.

Mary was to remain in the mystery of the compassion right up to the day of her Assumption. It is thus that she, as spouse and mother, experienced for the sake of the

Church the painful birth of her Son's Chosen People amid persecution and bloodshed. Even though she was to enter into glory without undergoing the corruption of the tomb, she was not allowed to live the glorious mysteries in a glorious and luminous fashion here below after the sorrowful mysteries had ended. The risen Jesus did not appear to her. Her last image of Jesus on earth was that of his face on the cross. Until the end of her life, she stayed at the foot of the cross, with St. John, the child of her tears. John would never be the child of her love in the way that Jesus was. As priest, he was indeed the sign and instrument of love, but not a sign which was at the same time the reality signified. He was rather like a living sacrament, giving her the Eucharistic presence of Jesus.

Many theologians suppose that the risen Jesus must have appeared to her privately, even though Scripture makes no mention of this. But she did not need such an apparition. The apostles did, both to revive their faith and to qualify them as public witnesses to the Resurrection. Mary undoubtedly experienced the grace of the Resurrection by a new infilling of the Holy Spirit; but it seems more probable that this was not accompanied by any external apparition.

Mary and the Destiny of the Universe

The figure of the Immaculate Virgin sheds a mysterious light on the meaning and destiny of the material universe. For there are two possible ways in which we can regard the universe. One is to view it as the object of scientific inquiry and technological development; the other is to reverence it as the abode of love. In the first way, the universe is an object for reason to investigate and exploit; in the second, it is a masterpiece of love, ordained to man's life of supernatural love — a life that requires an attitude of passivity to Infinite Love, an attitude of docility, littleness and humility.

This ambivalence is rooted ultimately in the matter of which the universe is composed. On the one hand, it is the subject of quantity, and of the physical properties founded on quantity. It is chiefly under the quantitative aspects of matter that human reason can grasp it, study its properties and realize its potential. On the other hand, matter is what enables Infinite Love to give the universe its 'human' dimensions, and make it the natural milieu for a community of living beings. This community in turn is centered on man and woman, and their eternal union in love. In the last analysis, the matter of which they are composed is what allows them to be formed by Infinite Love into an image of love.

From the first point of view, power, greatness and light are the chief values. The ancients considered the stars to be the noblest part of the universe, because they appeared to be perfect in form, full of light and unchanging, except for a circular movement that would continue forever. The medievals were tempted to view creation above all as a display of divine power and intelligence, and as a great work of art proportioned to the intellect of pure spirits, the angels. Although modern science has not sustained these views, it has discovered that the universe contains light, distance and magnitudes far surpassing anything ever imagined by the ancients. In its own way, it suggests that these are where the meaning of the universe is to be seen. In such a perspective, man's little planet, earth, is an insignificant speck. Even where an anthropocentric outlook is retained, the meaning and finality of human life are seen in the achievements of science and technology. Here too the ultimate measure of value tends to be bigness and complexity.

From the second point of view, the center and purpose of the universe lies in man. Not man as scientist or maker, but man who, as a meeting place of matter and spirit, has an unparalleled capacity for receiving and imaging forth Infinite Love. From this point of view, matter is seen as having been created for God's art of love. It does not appear as something inert and indifferent, but as the capacity to catch on fire, capacity for the passivity of love. God is then the Prime Mover, not as an agent or efficient cause, but as an end. The action of Infinite Love is an action of love, inspiring in the universe a movement of love. God attracts to himself a universe that gets its unity from, and subsists only in, this movement of love. But this movement is obscure for human reason, because both the Mover, Infinite Love, and the mobile, matter, elude the grasp of reason.

In this way of seeing things, what matters most about light is not its power to illumine (i.e., to be reflected by the quantified figures of things), but the invisible radiance by which it gives warmth. The warmth of the sun, absorbed by the earth, reemerges as life — a life that culminates in man. By his intellect, man is able to take cognizance of this natural movement of love which grace has supernaturalized.

According as he accepts or rejects the grace of love, man freely chooses between these two views of the universe. He can go the way of science, investigating the universe and working on it in a spirit of exploration, activity and independence. Or he can go the way of wisdom and love, which demands of him above all an attitude of passivity and receptivity in respect to Infinite Love. Instead of a spirit of action flowing from the desire for independence, it requires a humble acceptance of one's dependence. Here progress is not measured by greatness, but by littleness — the littleness proper to love. Here, man docilely and lovingly allows himself to be drawn by the Holy Spirit, not in the direction of greatness and quantity, but in that of recollection and loving intimacy.

The coming of Jesus made it clear that the universe was created and disposed primarily in view of love. His Incarnation was an incarnation of Divine Love. The Father sent him to reveal his love for us. By her example and by her silence, the Immaculate Virgin shows us the way Jesus wants his disciples to take. She teaches contemplatives in particular to accept the sacrifices implied by the hidden life (the sacrifice of earthly fame and knowledge), to plunge into a life of poverty and humility, under the aegis of the Holy Spirit, in order to prepare as fully and directly as possible for the final coming of Jesus, who, as Bridegroom, will bring the world to its fulfillment in love, complete its unity and restore it to the Father.

Supplementary Notes
(by the Editor)

Our Knowledge of Mary's Inner Life

Is it possible to write seriously about what went on in the mind and heart of the Mother of Jesus? Scripture tells us so very little even about her external activity; regarding her inner life, its chief assertion is simply that she had one. After the events at Bethlehem, we read, "Mary treasured up all these things and pondered them in her heart" (Luke 2:19). Twelve years later, the same theme is repeated: "His mother treasured all these things in her heart" (Luke 2:51). Beyond that, we know that she regarded herself as a handmaiden of the Lord (Luke 1:38), and that she seems to have resolved on a life of virginity (Luke 1:34) — something most exceptional at that time. She was troubled by the greeting of the angel and wondered what it might mean (Luke 1:29), but submitted wholeheartedly when the will of God was made known to her (Luke 1:38). She seems to have been rather silent, although we have the exultant hymn of praise and thanks to God that Luke places upon her lips (Luke 1:46-55). It is clear that her union with God did not dull her compassion for others in their moments of need (Elizabeth and the bridegroom of Cana: Luke 1:39 and John 2:3), nor her anxiety when the twelve-year-old Jesus got lost for three days (Luke 2:43). Neither did it give her an immediate understanding of Jesus' mysterious sayings (Luke 2:50).

But how are we to know what went on behind the silence with which she carried out her role in the birth and death of Jesus, and listened while he preached to the multitudes, debated with the crowds and was derided by his brethren (Mark 3:21-22)? Above all, who can inform us about her life before the Annunciation or after Pentecost? She was with the apostles and the other women in prayer when the Spirit descended in wind and flames (Acts 2:1-4); but though the disciples were then given new tongues in which to utter God's praises, we hear nothing from Mary but silence.

From this handful of indications is it possible to divine

anything reliable about the inner life of that most blessed among women? There is an art of poetic insight, with which gifted people are able to conjure up sometimes very plausibly what may have gone on in the private lives and personal emotions of great figures of history. The product of their art is the historical novel or a kind of long-distance psychoanalysis. As the reader might be inclined to suppose that the present book is somewhat akin to works of that sort, we would like in the strongest possible language to disavow any such kinship. What is offered here is the product of prayerful reflection, not of "creative imagination." This is not to suggest that the latter is evil or frivolous; we should be grateful for the inventiveness of artists who have done much to color the dullness of our lives and sharpen our perceptions. But the aim of the present essay is not to create a character but to contemplate a reality already created by God — the second most beautiful of all his creations. The method employed here is not that of psychological analysis, but spiritual discernment of a totally different type.

There is a discerning of the inner meaning of the facts recounted in Scripture that is much more real than fiction and much more penetrating than psychology. The personages of Sacred Scripture — Jesus himself preeminently, but others also after him, with Mary the first among them — are not only factors in the movement of Salvation History; they are also living words by which the Lord speaks to us. None of them are dumb accidents, flotsam and jetsam strewn along the coast of the Holy Land; they are full of life and meaning — a meaning that is intended for us by the Lord of history whose mysterious, all-embracing wisdom, while accepting the freedom and responsibility of his creatures, molds them into a message as truly as the director of a symphony blends myriad vibrations into a harmonious melody. And the same Spirit who inspires the Sacred Writings lives also in the heart of the believing reader, enlightening him and making him sensitive to the meaning therein inscribed. The author of the Book makes himself our personal tutor, patiently coaching us to decipher it.

The possibility of such a reading is based first of all on

the fact that the same life that was lived by Jesus, Mary and the saints is participated in by those who embrace Jesus in faith, and open themselves to his Spirit. Just as, in human existence, one who has lived profoundly is often able, without a word of explanation, to read the signs of human life in others — not only obvious smiles and tears, but the inaudible sigh, the almost imperceptible tension, the faintest recoil — so too the signs of the Spirit in Jesus, Mary and the others, can often be read, sometimes with very penetrating perspicacity, by those who live by that same Spirit.

Admittedly the interpretation of these signs cannot be achieved with complete firmness and objectivity. Signs are not as determinate as words; hence the experience, intuition and personal involvement of the interpreter plays a much greater role in their interpretation. There will therefore always be differences of opinion about the significance of many events in Sacred History. The debate about how much Mary understood at the Annunciation is almost classical; the meaning of her role at Cana and Calvary is liable to various readings. This does not mean that the interpretation is purely subjective, but that it lays great demands upon the interpreter. For example, anyone who has no spiritual life of his own is ipso facto incapable of understanding many things in a life that was the personification and quintessence of Christian spirituality.

No claim to dogmatic certitude is made for the views expressed in the present book. They are offered for the reader to consider and evaluate in the light of his own insights. But they represent an earnest inquiry into the real meaning of the Mother of Jesus, not an essay in poetry. And, let us not overlook the fact that the very exercise of meditating on Mary, and the loving effort to know her better, even when it leads only to a certain plausibility, is itself a fruitful and salutary way to grow in personal relationship with this most enchanting, lovely and mysterious member of God's household.

Furthermore, the danger of subjectivity is mightily offset by the fact that the Church as a whole and especially the saints have been engaged for many centuries in this reflection. What could seem at first mere personal fancy acquires more and more authority when it is repeatedly and consistently reaffirmed by the common sentiment of God's prophetic people.

Another source for the understanding of particular biblical figures consists in the major doctrines of the faith and themes of Scripture. They furnish a perspective in which seemingly slight details sometimes take on surprising significance. Thus, Mary's affirmation of her virginity must be viewed in the light of the teachings of Jesus and Paul about virginity (not of course as though she was guided by them, but because they explain the meaning of that consecration of self which she was inspired to make). On a broader scale, the great doctrines of sin and grace, of redemption and resurrection, compose the essential framework in which everything about Mary must be situated.

On some points, the application of these doctrines to the instance of Mary has been defined by the Church in a way that enables us to rely on them with complete assurance — for example, that she came into the world untouched by the sinfulness that is endemic to human nature in its actual state; and that, on leaving this world, she entered immediately and fully into the glory of the restoration for which the rest of us must await the parousia. These doctrines provide a fulcrum for the interpretation of others. If Mary was free of the sin that hampers the rest of us humans, puzzling our resolves and hamstringing our undertakings, then her Yes at the Annunciation had a totality and firmness of which we are incapable; she was a pure exemplar of humanity elevated by grace. This simplifies the understanding of Mary, because it means that she had the purity of a full and perfect realization of the Christian ideal, unclouded by the murkiness and unintelligibility of evil. The theology of Mary is the finest instance of spiritual theology.

But this also creates another kind of problem for our naïve attempts to read the soul of the Mother of God. We have no experience of a life totally surrendered to the touch of the Spirit. It would, therefore, be a serious mistake for us to try to 'imagine' Mary's sentiments. And it would be lacking in sensitivity to a great mystery of faith to try to define her reactions and understanding of things by the mentality of "the average Jewish girl of her epoch." Whatever else Mary was, she was not average, she was eminent. For comparisons that may at least remotely orient our study of her life, it is to the mystics we must look. In fact, mystical experience, understood as a privileged but authentic fulfillment of that life in the Spirit which is common to all believers, has been taken as a major guideline for the sketch (not portrait!) that is offered here.

Mary as the Bride of Christ

There are several difficult themes in this book about which it might be helpful to say a word of explanation: the presentation of Mary as Bride of Christ; the passive and dependent attitude attributed to her; and finally, the interpretation made of her interiority.

Calling Mary the Bride of Christ is not just a sentimental touch that could readily be dispensed with; it is crucial to the interpretation of Mary offered in the foregoing pages. Perhaps a brief explanation here will eliminate any suggestion of an unnatural relationship between Jesus and his mother and show that the notion of Mary as Bride of Christ, difficult though it be, is both orthodox and intelligible.

In the first place, it is very traditional. Mary was already presented as Bride of Christ during the fifth century by Ephraem the Syrian, but not again apparently until a sermon composed some time before 800 (PG 43:485-501). There are, however, meanwhile vague references to Mary as spouse of God. In the Latin Church, the notion of Mary as spouse of Christ came into vogue during the twelfth century, and was accepted and discreetly employed by such solid theologians and doctors of the Church as St. Bernard (1090-1153), Aelred of Rielvaux (1109-1167), St. Albert the Great (1200-1280), and St. Bonaventure (1221-1274). Those who used and developed it most were Rupert of Deutz (c. 1070-c. 1130), Herman of Tournai (d. after 1147), Amadeus of Lausanne (c. 1110-1159) and Philip of Harvengt (d. 1183). It remained a fairly strong theme in Marian piety until the sixteenth century and was still abundantly employed by St. Lawrence of Brindisi (1559-1619). Under the withering scorn of the Reformation and especially the Enlightenment, however, it began to retreat, until it disappeared almost entirely. In the last century, Scheeben (1835-1888) made a powerful but unsuccessful effort to revive it, placing the bridal motherhood at the focal point of his theology of Mary. Serge Boulgakov (d. 1944), one of the most influential Orthodox theologians of the present century, also speaks of Mary as the Mother and Bride of the Word of God.[40]

To put the sense of this appellation in perspective, we should recall that Israel was seen as the bride of God in the Old Testament. In Christian eyes, Mary is regarded as the culmination of Israel, the Daughter of Sion par excellence, and therefore the one in whom Israel's bridal role was perfectly and most personally realized. It is this that gives sense and meaning to her "vow of virginity," discussed in chapter 4. God and God alone was the spouse to whom she devoted her heart and her whole being exclusively. Moreover, the fact that she was Mother of the Son of God gave a rationale for thinking of her as the bride of God the Father, a theme developed by M. Olier (1608-1657). And the fact that she conceived through the overshadowing of the Holy Spirit has often led Christian tradition to visualize her as the bride of the Holy Spirit.

But the Christian virgin is not just a spouse of God, she is in particular the bride of Christ. In her, the vocation of the Church, the New Israel, as Bride of the Lamb (Apocalypse 21:9) is realized personally. In such a perspective, it is inevitable that Mary, who has always been seen as the model of Christian virgins and the preeminent type of the Church, should also be regarded as the Bride of Christ par excellence.

This logic of metaphors might not suffice by itself to outweigh the objection that it is unbecoming to speak of Jesus' mother as his bride. But there are grounds much more direct and central than the above reasonings for viewing Mary in this way. In its effort to express the extraordinary intensity of Mary's love for Jesus, Christian piety has sensed that the natural love of a mother for her child, strong and beautiful as it is, does not adequately

166

represent it. Mary did not merely receive Jesus with affection as any mother does her child; she embraced him and his mission with a deliberate and voluntary decision that is more like that of a bride for her husband.

Human love has many modulations. The love of a mother for her child, and that of a bride for her husband, are two characteristically different types of love, corresponding to the difference between natural affection and voluntary choice. Maternal love is based on a preexisting natural bond, and springs from it. Spousal love is a free, personal act that creates a bond of its own. Mary had, to be sure, a natural maternal love for her Son; she had it with a purity and intensity surpassing that of any other mother, because the grace of her Immaculate Conception freed her affections from any taint of selfishness. But Jesus was not just an ordinary son. He was in the unique situation of being a son who freely chose his mother. By that sovereignty belonging to his divinity, the Son of God freely selected the woman through whom he was to enter into this world. Mary, in turn, was the only mother ever in a position to accept a definite individual as her son. The angel of the Annunciation did not merely announce that she was about to become pregnant; he identified the proffered child as Son of God and Messiah ("Son of David"). Mary freely consented to this proposal. Thus Jesus and Mary entered into their mother-child relationship by a conscious acceptance of each other. This is the objective basis for holding that the love between them is not adequately understood as the natural affection between mother and child, but had also the character of free, deliberate choice that is found in spousal love.

Moreover, as the Second Eve, summoned to take her stand beside the New Adam, Mary wholeheartedly embraced and espoused the mission on which he was sent and the sacrifice in which it culminated. She was not merely a mother following with fond affection and anxious concern the development of her son's career; actively, deliberately and voluntarily she concurred in it. His "Thy will be done" was ratified by the Amen of her heart, prolonging the Fiat originally directed to the angel. It is characteristic of the bride, rather than of the mother as such, freely and by an act of choice to take the work and person of her Man as the form and focus of her own life. Other mothers too, no doubt, have also devoted themselves to the career of their sons by a deliberate, voluntary acceptance that goes beyond the simple affection of motherhood. Of them too it may be appropriate to say that something of a spousal note, over and above the maternal one, marks their relationships to their sons. What Tradition says of Mary is that such was eminently the case with her. She loved Jesus as the most devoted of mothers loving the finest of sons; but there was also in her love an intensity, a fire and a free deliberate choice that belong more to the spouse than to the mother.

Mary's Passivity and Dependence

Another topic requiring discussion is the attitude of passivity and dependence attributed to Mary. Psychologists have given a bad name to passive, dependent characters. There is considerable truth in their estimate, but often it is crudely oversimplified. Happily, some currents of thought today are restoring the balance by reaffirming the factors of receptivity and trust which are indispensable to human equilibrium. So far as the spiritual life is concerned, three points need to be made. First, that man's primordial posture in regard to God is one of receptivity. With our fellow human beings, there is an interchange which is ideally an equal blend of giving and receiving; but in regard to God, we are totally recipients, and we have nothing to give or to do that we have not first received from him. To try to be autonomously active is to chop the very roots of our action. However, adults are not usually conscious of this fact. They have long cultivated an active psychology, focused on what they are doing or ought to do. Only through much stripping, purification and experience can we be brought to appreciate the role of passivity and receptivity in regard to God.

Secondly, the action of the Prime Mover does not make us puppets. God not only respects, he creates our freedom and responsibility. The saints are people of astonishing strength, liberty and resourcefulness; but this is so only because they have first opened the interior floodgates that allow them to be permeated by the action of the Holy Spirit.

Third, the passivity and dependence of the saints, and of Mary above all others, is a matter not only of ontological objectivity, but of personal love. Reliance on the loved one is a joyous thing for the lover, and a stimulus to love itself. One of the serious damages inflicted on modern life by heavy-handed psychologizing is the anxiety so many have about becoming too dependent on those they love. No doubt there is a relationship of domination/enslavement, and there is a sickly atrophy of the aggressive faculty, both of which are parasites on and corruptions of love. But excessive anxiety about these caricatures can inhibit the willingly accepted need of the other that is inherent in human love itself. A woman's need for the strength and protection of her husband, or his need of her tenderness and affection, when consciously and gladly accepted, do not degrade but confirm their love. With still more reason, the saint not only submits to, but willingly embraces, his dependence on God, as an occasion to glorify him. It was not a servile heart but one spontaneous and free that sang: "My spirit rejoices in God my Savior . . . for the Mighty One has done great things for me. . ." (Luke 1:47, 49). The God from whom she received all things was also the Beloved to whom her heart was wholly given. To receive from him added to her joy.

Mary's Interiority

Not many years ago, the very idea of interior life was scorned by a popular psychology that regarded "extraversion" as synonymous with wholesomeness and maturity. All forms of turning inward were treated indiscriminately as perverse or immature. Echoes of this attitude can still be heard in pop spirituality. But the revival of serious interest in prayer and spirituality during the past ten or twenty years has combined with many efforts to synthesize traditional spirituality with modern psychology. Many of these syntheses have been further colored by methods of meditation derived from the Far East. The confluence of these three currents has given new respectability to the notions of interiority and interior life.

However, the interiority so conceived is likely to be one of psychological introspection and self-analysis, often heavily laden with dream interpretation. Here is not the place to appraise so complex a subject; let me say merely that it is often easier to defend interior life against the crass old contempt than against this ambivalent new popularity. Formerly it was enough to point out the simple distinction between morbid introspection and healthy self-possession. Now it is necessary to explain that the interior life spoken of in the spiritual tradition that goes back at least as far as St. Augustine is totally different from that of the psychologists, the meditators or even the poets. It belongs to a dimension of the human spirit that remains completely unknown until the breath and the touch of the Holy Spirit have awakened us to it. Compared to it, the 'inner world' of the philosopher, the poet or the psychologist is quite exterior. The cultivated introspection of these latter, although it can, when rightly used, be an aid to the interior life, is more often an obstacle, all the more so because of the danger of being confused with it.

Notes

1. St. Thomas Aquinas, *Summa Theologiae*, I, 20, 1; I-II, 23, 4; 25, 2.
2. The two paragraphs in italics are the work of the editor.
3. If human consciousness begins in the womb before birth, its dependence on the sense of touch is in that case even more obvious.
4. According to the common teaching of spiritual writers going back as far as the sixth century, the spiritual life develops in three phases, first the purgative, then the illuminative, and finally the unitive. For an extensive survey of the classical doctrine, see R. Garrigou-Lagrange, *The Three Ages of the Interior Life* (London & St. Louis: London, 1948).
5. Likewise, the Gifts of the Holy Spirit are not given merely to help us practice the moral virtues, or to make us attain our natural ends with a supernatural spirit and orientation. In the plan of God, they are given above all so that the theological virtues, especially charity, may develop connaturally and reach fulfillment even here on earth. They are given, in other words, to enable our lives to be not only ordained to God as their last end, but actually lived immediately and totally in his presence, in a real union with him. (T.P.)
6. The author is articulating in theological language a contrast that Mary would not, of course, have conceptualized in such terms, but which she would have sensed acutely.
7. Cf. St. Thomas, *Summa Theologiae*, II-II, 141, 5.
8. "Prime matter" is a philosophical concept, not to be identified with the concept of matter employed in physics and chemistry. It was Aristotle who first argued from the fact that a thing can be turned into something else of an essentially different nature (e.g., the food we eat being assimilated into our bodies) to the conclusion that underlying all empirically observable beings, there must be an ultimate stuff or material, having absolutely no quantity,

quality or characteristics of any sort, but only the sheer potentiality of becoming anything in the material order. St. Thomas, and after him the whole Thomistic school, as well as most other schools of scholastic theology, assumed this principle, which is still defended by Thomists today. How this philosophical concept of matter relates to the atomic structure of matter as disclosed by the empirical sciences is one of the crucial problems of Thomistic philosophy of nature today, but does not concern us here.

9. Celibacy and other forms of asceticism have been practiced for religious and philosophical motives in other cultures, notably Hinduism and Buddhism, and even in pre-Christian Judaism (by the Essenes). However, the evangelical counsels, i.e., poverty, chastity and obedience, cultivated in imitation of Jesus and according to his recommendation, have a very different sense and spirit from these other forms of asceticism, as will appear in the course of this chapter.

10. The paragraph in italics is the work of the editor. I must add in all honesty that once when I pointed out to Father Philippe that no modern scholar would admit the historicity of Mary's Presentation, he accepted that without protest. However, I later heard him speaking about it again as a real event, so I really don't know how he would feel about my inserting this paragraph.

11. *Summa Theologiae*, III, 29, 2.

12. The remark in the parentheses is the work of the editor.

13. Not that the bodies of the dead are in no way loved by God, but simply that the dead body does not participate in that complete love which implies reciprocity.

14. See his Commentary on the *Nichomachean Ethics* of Aristotle, III, 7 and 9 (lect. xv, No. 551 and lect. xviii, No. 589).

15. *Summa Theologiae*, II-II, 123, 8.

16. The sending of the Holy Spirit into the world under

the figure of tongues of fire is called his visible mission. Being infused into human hearts in the form of grace is his invisible mission. Similarly, in the case of the Son, there was a visible mission, namely the Incarnation; the Son's invisible mission is identical with that of the Spirit.

17. Cf. chapter 8, note 3.
18. Tradition has taken this name from Isaiah 14:12.
19. *Summa Theologiae*, II-II, 173, 4.
20. Cf. Vatican II, Constitution on the Church, No. 62.
21a, b. The paragraphs in italics are the work of the editor.
22. This has been common doctrine in the Church for many centuries. Cf. St. Thomas, *Summa Theologiae*, III, 9, 2; 10; and 34, 4, based on a tradition that was established long before the time of St. Thomas. Pius XII reaffirmed this doctrine in the Encyclical *Mystici Corporis* (cf. Denzinger-Schönmetzer, 3812; note also the Decree of the Holy Office of 1918, *ibid.*, 3645).

   During the past few decades, an impulse to make Jesus more like us in his humanity has led many theologians to reject or modify considerably the thesis of Christ's beatific knowledge. The most famous of these attempts (and one of the more moderate) is that of Karl Rahner in *Theological Investigations* V, 193-215; "Dogmatic reflections on the knowledge and self-consciousness of Christ." This is not the place to go into a discussion of these views, which do not seem to do sufficient justice either to the Gospel portrait of Jesus (especially that of St. John) or to the exigencies of the Hypostatic Union. Most of them, moreover, fail to appreciate the finesse of the Thomistic theory, which allows for a fully authentic human existence in Jesus. But for the purpose of these present reflections, traditional doctrine will simply be assumed.
23. St. Thomas, *ibid.*, Q. 7.
24. *Ibid.*, Qq. 9-11. It is, of course, Jesus in his earthly existence that is under consideration here, not the Divine Word as such.

25. Cf. chapter 8, note 2.
26. Strictly speaking, Jesus did not have a public life, insofar as life implies a certain permanence and stability. There was merely a public ministry as an element of his life. This touches a very mysterious aspect of Jesus' mission. (T.P.)
27. *Summa Theologiae*, III, 42, 4.
28. The sacraments are part of the liturgy, indeed its principal part. But the liturgy includes also other acts of Church worship, such as the Divine Office, that are not sacraments.
29. The progress of technology enables us to perceive more and more acutely the difference between the natural and the artificial. Unlike the achievements of our technology, that which is natural arises from the dispositions that God himself, by his art of love, has put into nature. Should not all our modern discoveries serve as humble instruments and occasions for us to enter more deeply into the mystery of our faith, and especially the mystery of the Incarnation, the *chef d'oeuvre* produced by God out of created matter? (T.P.)

    If a physicist were to maintain that the properties of 'natural' light could be duplicated artificially, at least under certain theoretical conditions, that would not affect the present argument, which is concerned with the light actually found in nature, compared to the light actually produced by our technology. And it is obviously not the author's purpose to analyze light in the way proper to the physical sciences, but simply to discern its theological and religious meaning as factor in the world of man. (E.O'C.)
30. The paragraphs in italics are the work of the editor.
31. Pius IX, *Ineffabilis Deus* (*Acta Pii IX*, Pars I, vol. 1) p. 599.
32. There is no contradiction or incompatibility about speaking here of the Holy Spirit as her spouse, whereas above Jesus is represented in that role. Jesus and his Spirit are fully one, both in their love for Mary and in her love for them.
33. See especially Daniel 7:13.

34. It is chiefly by grace and glory that man is the image and likeness of God. Cf. St. Thomas, *Summa Theologiae*, I, 93, 4.
35. *Legatus Divinae Pietatis*, Solemnes ed. (Poitiers & Paris, 1975), Book IV, ch. 4. Cf. *The Life and Revelations of St. Gertrude* (Westminster, MD: Newman Press, 1949), p. 316.
36. Such a supposition does not conflict with Jesus' statement that "the Son of Man has no place to lay his head" (Matthew 8:20). This statement was not meant in a strictly literal sense, as we can see from the reference to Jesus' dwelling place at Capharnaum in John 1:38.
37. Earlier, John was said to be entrusted to Mary; here it is the reverse. Externally and socially, John was to care for Mary; but on the plane of the hidden and interior life, he was her pupil.
38. We speak here of reason functioning strictly as reason, not in its more primal function as intellect, which is of course presupposed by love.
39. The contrast made here does not imply that the scientific outlook is wrong, or that it is incompatible with that of the divine wisdom of love. One whose mentality is molded basically by the wisdom of love can very well assimilate science and technology into it. The converse, however, does not hold. The crucial question is, which outlook is dominant in a person's mentality.
40. Cf. D. Flanagan, "The image of the bride in the earlier Marian tradition," *Irish Theological Quarterly* 27 (1960), 111-124, and "Mary, Bride of Christ," ibid. 28 (1961), 233-237; Michael O'Carroll, "Spouse of God (Bride of God), Mary as," in his *Theotokos*, Wilmington, Glazier, 1982. For more detail, see *Mary: A History of Doctrine and Devotion*, by Hilda Graef (New York: Sheed and Ward, 1963, 1965). While by no means an adequate treatment of the theme, this work supplies enough examples for our present purposes.